A GRIM ALMANAC OF

CAMBRIDGESHIRE

A GRIM ALMANAC OF

CAMBRIDGESHIRE

N E I L   R .   S T O R E Y

For Rosie

Frontispiece: Storm clouds rolling over the Black Fens near Isleham.

First published 2009

The History Press
The Mill, Brimscombe Port
Stroud, Gloucestershire, GL5 2QG
www.thehistorypress.co.uk

British Library Cataloguing in Publication Data.
A catalogue record for this book is available from the British Library.

ISBN 978 0 7524 5010 0

Typesetting and origination by The History Press
Printed in India by Nutech Print Services

CONTENTS

ACKNOWLEDGEMENTS

In my travels for this book it has been proved, yet again, that you meet some of the nicest people when researching the grimmest tales. There really are too many to mention all by name, but I wish to record particular thanks to the following: Stewart and Rosie Evans; Robert Bell; Wisbech and Fenland Museum; Mike Petty; the Norris Museum, Huntingdon; Burwell Museum; G. David Booksellers, Cambridge; Cambridge Libraries and Information Service; Wisbech Tourist Information Centre; Peterborough Cathedral; Dr Stephen Cherry; Alan Murdie; Sarah Oldfield and the Whittlesea Straw Bearers; Whittlesey Museum; Les Bolland; Clifford Elmer Books; Robert 'Bookman' Wright, Elaine Abel; and I remember, with affection, the late David Ferrow.

I also record my thanks to my wonderful students for their interest and comments, and last but by no means least thank my family, especially my darling Molly and my son Lawrence for their enduring love, support and interest in my research.

PICTURE CREDITS

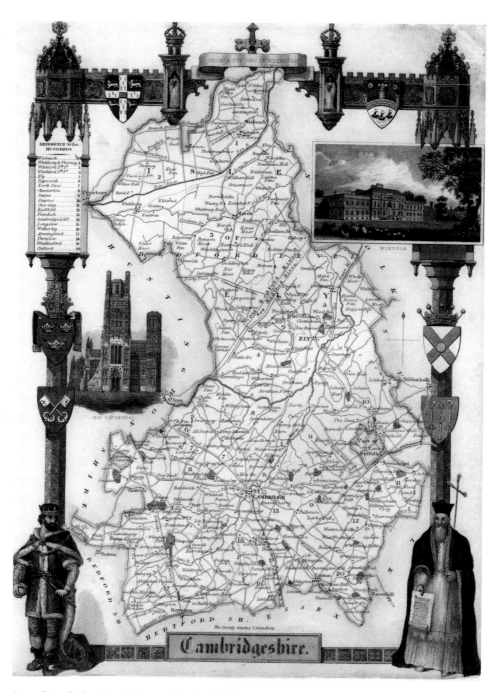

Map of Cambridgeshire by Thomas Moule, 1838.

INTRODUCTION

Truth is always strange,
Stranger than fiction.

Lord Byron, *Don Juan* (1823)

Cambridgeshire is a county of remarkable contrasts; here can be found one of our nations' greatest and longest-established seats of learning, surrounded by countryside and Fens where belief in the old ways of cunning folk and witchcraft have lingered far longer than in many other counties and is still spoken of in some rural areas with the hushed tones and caution accorded to a living belief. Fen folk were a breed apart who worked hard and lived their lives surrounded by their own lore and legend. In his *Britannia* (1586), William Camden described them as 'a kind of people according to the nature of the place where they dwell, rude, uncivil and envious to all other whom they call Upland Men; who stalking high upon stilts apply their minds to grazing, fishing and fowling.' Woe betide any outsider, especially 'adventurers' and their workmen, who would attempt to interfere with these peoples' lives by embanking, ditching and building sluices. The Fen Tigers acquired a fearsome reputation for using any means to preserve their way of life; the labours of the outsiders by day would often be destroyed by Fen Tigers overnight. An outsider workman or other official, be they bailiff or lawman, who lingered in the Fens after dark tempted fate; I have read and been told during my research that there are 'many more bodies sunk in those Fens than anyone will ever know.'

If hard times came or offence was caused to the working folk of the Cambridgeshire countryside they were not slow in making their dissatisfaction known to their masters. Incendiarism rose to epidemic proportions in the nineteenth century, the story of the Littleport Riot of 1816 is still known to many, but as the pages in this book will show, although the scale and drama of that protest was exceptional, over the years, before and long after Littleport, the mobs gathered and marched many more times across Cambridgeshire.

During my travels across East Anglia investigating and collecting the stories for my *Grim Almanac* books I have found, in every county, the surface can be scratched and soon the pus and festered corruption of the darker side of human nature can soon be squeezed out from the annals of its past. Although they drew great fascination and curiosity at the time, many of the stories in this volume have not been recounted for generations. This book is a journey through some of the darkest moments of Cambridgeshire's past, but alongside this cornucopia of crime, punishments, death, disaster, cunning folk and witches, are tales of heroes, wonders and curiosities – especially giants; I have never found quite so many in one county. A potent blend indeed, once undoubtedly washed down with poppy tea, a brew well known across the county and harvested locally from the swaying white opium poppies that once punctuated the Cambridgeshire landscape.

Read on dear reader, if you dare ...

Neil R. Storey, 2009

One of the droves on Quy Fen, near where William Ison lost his life in 1873.

JANUARY

PROCESSION OF THE PLOUGH ON PLOUGH MONDAY.

Plough Monday celebrations, the traditional start of the English agricultural year once marked in every Cambridgeshire village and town on the first Monday after Epiphany.

1 JANUARY 1631

Hobson's Choice, well probably not. On this day Thomas Hobson died – one of the few instances where *he* really had no choice. Hobson (b. 1544) was a carrier who ran the mail between London and Cambridge. He maintained a livery stable outside the gates of St Catharine's College and would lease his horses, when not being used for his carrier purposes, to students and masters at the university. His best horses were in regular demand and soon became overworked, so he adopted an unwavering rotation system by which he refused to allow any horse to be taken from his stables except in its proper turn – if you didn't want the horse offered to you the other option would be made clear – 'this one or none', in other words take it or leave it, thus Hobson's Choice!

2 JANUARY 1864

The last public execution in Cambridgeshire. John Green (25) lived with his wife and three young children in Whittlesea and worked in the local malt house. He had been drinking heavily when he encountered Elizabeth Brown (36) a woman 'of bad character and intemperate habits.' At about 1 a.m., Green and Brown snuck into the warm kiln of the malt house where Green worked. After more drink and talk Green made a sexual advance towards Brown, but she denied him. Green flew at her, grabbed her throat and

Thomas Hobson, 1544–1631.

12

dragged her to the floor where he beat her unconscious with his punches and kicks. Thinking he had killed her, Green then panicked and attempted to dispose of the body in the furnace. It would not fit, so he attempted to smash parts of her body, but still it would not go through the doors, so he found some sacks, wrapped them around her body, and threw a shovel of cinders on top to ignite them and watched the body burn. At five in the morning Green's friend, William Smedley, came to start work at the malting kiln and discovered the still smouldering remains. Curiously, he took an hour to raise the alarm. Alarmingly, the post-mortem revealed Elizabeth had not died from the beating but rather from asphyxiation caused by the fire. Smedley and Green were both arrested; Green charged with murder and Smedley with being an accessory to murder and arson. Smedley was acquitted, but Green was found guilty and deservedly received no mercy. On 1 January 1864, Messrs Bell & Son erected the gallows outside the County Gaol. At two minutes before nine on Saturday 2 January 1864 Green was brought onto the scaffold wearing a white smock, red handkerchief, corduroy trousers, hat and heavy nailed boots. Once positioned on the gallows trap, his hat was replaced with a white hood, the noose was adjusted and he was launched into eternity.

3 JANUARY John Howard Reports on the Prisons of Cambridgeshire & Huntingdon

The County Gaol at Huntingdon, 1782. Gaoler John Randall:

This gaol is also the County Bridewell and Town Gaol. For debtors, a day room or kitchen and over it a large lodging-room. Near it is a day-room for felons and down nine steps a dungeon for men-felons in which is a small room for the condemned. In another place, down 7 steps, is a dungeon for women-felons; the floor of it is level with the court, in which is the bridewell. This has two rooms below for men and two above for women. No chimneys. The prison and court are too small but I always found the whole remarkably clean, except at my visit in 1779. Clauses against spirituous liquors hung up. The Act for preserving the health of prisoners is not hung up. No infirmary. No bath. Salary for the bridewell £24 16s; for the town gaol £4 plus £4 16 a year for straw ...

Howard also recorded:

I was sorry to hear at my visit in 1776, that Mr Brock, the late chaplain, who officiated very consistently twice a week and had a salary of only £20 was dismissed. He would have continued his attendance, without the salary, but an order was made expressly forbidding it.

4 JANUARY 1884

Prize fight over two counties. James Hayes (22), labourer and Robert Webb, a tailor were brought before the Cambridgeshire Quarter Sessions charged with common assault, where they both pleaded 'guilty'; they were in fact the combatants in a prize fight. Such activity was against the law so an ideal place for such contests was the area of the borders between Cambridgeshire and Suffolk, where if one constabulary attempted to arrest those concerned, they only had to step over the border to avoid capture by that particular county's police force. During the hearing the court was reminded by Dr Cooper for prosecution of a similar incident some thirty years before on the same spot, and he asked the court not to pass a nominal sentence but rather one that would deter anyone tempted to repeat the offence. However, the Bench were aware the accused had been in gaol since October of the previous year and so only sentenced both men to seven days' imprisonment.

5 JANUARY 1831

Charles Fowler and Johnson Smith were brought before the Sessions in Wisbech. Fowler, a chair-mender by trade, and Irishman Smith were bodysnatchers. They had built a lucrative business robbing graves in the dead of night in Ely and its surrounding villages, but their luck ran out after stealing the body of Rebecca Shearman from St Mary's churchyard. They packed the corpse into a hamper and took it to the wagon office of Marsh & Swan to arrange conveyance to London. The office clerk's suspicions were raised by the horrible smell emitting from the hamper; he called the constables and soon Fowler and Smith were under arrest. Found guilty of desecrating the grave of Rebecca Shearman, both were sentenced to twelve months' hard labour in the House of Correction.

6 JANUARY 1899

Harry Vere Hargreaves (17) began the first full day of his prison sentence after being brought before Peterborough Quarter Sessions charged with obtaining food and lodging by false pretences. Hargreaves had run away from his home in New Zealand the previous year. On his arrival in this country he lived by his wits, successively occupying and running out of rooms in London. After escaping to Torquay, he was brought before magistrates and was sent to a Church of England home – from which he promptly made his escape. He next appeared at Peterborough, having answered an advertisement by a Mrs Morling of Werrington Hall for a paying guest. He then went to Eastbourne where he served two months for obtaining board and lodging by false pretences. Caught again and brought up at Peterborough, Hargreaves was given twenty-eight weeks' imprisonment, after which his father paid his passage back home tp New Zeland.

7 JANUARY 1536

Catherine of Aragon, first wife of Henry VIII, dies at Kimbolton Castle. She had continued to refer to herself as Henry's only lawfully-wedded wife and England's only rightful Queen Consort and her loyal servants continued to address her by that title. Brought to the decaying and remote Kimbolton Castle in 1535, Catherine was in poor health; modern medical experts suggest she was suffering from cancer, but she lived with the suspicion that she was being poisoned under the orders of Henry. She confined herself to one room, fasted for most of the time, and only left her quarters to attend Mass. Wearing the hair shirt of the Order of St Francis, she prepared to meet her end. Catherine was buried in Peterborough Cathedral as a Dowager Princess of Wales, not a Queen. Henry was not present at her funeral, he also forbade her daughter, Mary, to attend. Her ghost is said to haunt the chamber where she died.

8 JANUARY Strange Tales and Folklore of Cambridgeshire: Lantern Men

After dark, fenland can take on a very different atmosphere; sometimes one of foreboding and certainly one of danger for those who would dare to cross the Fens by moonlight because they may well be led astray and to their watery doom by the ghostly glow of the Lantern Men, otherwise known as 'Hytersprites', 'Jack-a-Lanterns' or 'Will o' the Wisp', These strange lights have been recorded many times all over the Fens; some say they are simply self-igniting marsh gas, while others believe they are the souls or spirits of drowned men rising up again after dark. The ghosts of the drowned are said to rise up in daylight on one day of the year in particular – at the first light of dawn on May Day.

Catherine of Aragon.

9 JANUARY 1838

The gaoler of Huntingdon County Gaol was away escorting a number of convicts to London, when Thomas Godwin, who had been imprisoned for debt, saw his chance and managed to get up and over the prison wall; the rope, thought to have been bought by his mother Anne and smuggled into the prison, was found hanging on the outside wall. Anne Godwin was brought to trial and faced fourteen years' transportation if found guilty, but the judge, Mr Baron Parke, decided there was no solid proof against her and she was acquitted. By the time of his mother's appearance at the assizes, Thomas Godwin was long gone.

10 JANUARY

Plough Monday. On or about this date (the first Monday after Epiphany) falls Plough Monday. The plough would be blessed, often in a church, and then taken out to the field where many local lads would be initiated as plough boys or plough 'jags'. This involved the boys kneeling on the field near the plough, and removing their hats the old ploughman would then knock the bottom of their boots with his 'witch bone'. Once initiated the boys would black their faces, deck themselves in ribbons, and take a 'fool plough' (usually an old hand plough dragged out from a farm yard) around the town or village and 'holla largesse' (a gift of money, beer or food) from door-to-door. Those who sent the boys away with a flea in their ear ran the risk of having their path or lawn ploughed up! In Whittlesea their celebrations included the 'Straw Bear', a creation that was constructed with great lengths of tightly twisted straw bands wound up the arms, legs and body of the man or boy who was unfortunate enough to have been chosen for this honour. The 'bear' would then clumsily walk around Whittlesea and was made to dance in front of houses for largesse. Local folk took a great pride in this festival; the straw for the beast was carefully selected each year, only the best available would do – the harvesters saying, 'That'll do for the Bear.' In 1909 a local police inspector put a stop to the 'cadging' by the bear and the festival died off until it was revived again in 1980 by the Whittlesey Society.

11 JANUARY 1831

An inquest was held on this day at the Rose & Crown Inn, Wisbech, upon the body of John Turner, a farmer from Upwell who had been found dead in a dyke by Mr Lilley's field near New Common Bridge, near Wisbech. Mr Turner appeared to have been robbed, but his death was caused by 'some delirious drug having been given him or by some other diabolical means.' After deliberating for over twenty-three hours, the jury returned a verdict of 'how he came to his death is unknown.'

12 JANUARY 1738

Notorious highwayman Dick Turpin took refuge in the Three Tuns pub in Cambridge. After Turpin's execution at York in 1739, a glass case containing his hat, cravat, coat, doublet, mask, pistol and spurs was displayed in the pub for many years afterwards; the following notice was displayed alongside:

> Be it known to all ye Goodselves That here do come to drink of my Good Beer or to those that do Here Come to Tarry and for to rest their Goodselves and Horses for the night that the clothes Here Set once were belonged to Dick Turpin the famous Highway Robber. He on the eve of January 12th 1738 Did'st put up at this Goodly inn as often he did but alack he was sudden surprised by Runners and did have at quick to go just as he was and with only his horse leaving behind his other chattels in my care.

This remarkable display became part of the now defunct Cambridge Museum of Prison, Punishment and Royal Relics on Trumpington Street (*see* 28 December).

13 JANUARY 1911

At the Huntingdon Assizes before Mr Justice Ridley, twelve men were charged with rioting at Yaxley during the North Huntingdon election. The disturbance occurred at a Unionist meeting in the village schoolroom on 15 December 1910, when it was alleged some thirty or forty Peterborough unionists were set upon by between 300–400 men, women and children; sticks were used and stones were thrown. Mr Dickens for the defence admitted there was a riot but said that fortunately no serious injury was done to persons or property. Four of the defendants were found 'not guilty'; eight others pleaded 'guilty' and were bound over to keep the peace. Mr Justice Ridley strongly condemned such interference with political opponents as had occurred.

The Whittlesea Straw Bear and his keeper, 1909.

Dick Turpin, the notorious highwayman, who was a frequent visitor to the roads of Cambridgeshire.

14 JANUARY 1902

End of the Cambridge pornographer. Detective Inspector Arrow and Detective Sergeant Badcock from New Scotland Yard entered a well-furnished rented house called 'Edenfield' on Trumpington Road, Cambridge armed with a warrant for the arrest of Dr Sinclair Roland (a.k.a. De Villiers) who was charged with conspiring to print, sell and publish obscene books, pictures and pamphlets. The women in the house (also charged with similar offences), when asked where Roland was, claimed he was away in London; the detectives were not convinced and conducted a search of the house. After searching for over two hours, a very large wash stand was moved from against the wall of the billiard room at the top of the house; behind it was a small door inside which was a dummy cupboard, barricaded at the back with large trunks and kept in position by three iron rods and a number of heavy planks. Crawling through the aperture, Detective Sergeant Badcock found it led to another room, in one of the walls of which there was a similar door. Forced open Sinclair Roland was discovered inside, crouching against the rafters of the roof. He was conveyed to Cambridge police station, but died about an hour later having secretly taken poison.

15 JANUARY 1906

Samuel Poulter (38) was brought before the Cambridge Assizes indicted for the wilful murder of his wife Julia at Kirtling on 23 December. Poulter, a butcher, claimed his wife had insulted him. Poulter was known to fly into rages and storm outside shooting at nothing in particular. He claimed he had stepped into the orchard, tripped and the gun went off; he saw his wife fall in the nearby yard. Poulter did not run to her, instead he calmly walked back to the house and sent one of his children to tell a neighbour while he waited in the house for the police to arrive. At his trial, Poulter was found guilty, but the recommended mercy on the grounds that he had acted under the influence of alcohol. The judge, Mr Justice Lawrence, told the prisoner that he had rightly been found guilty of 'a bad and cruel murder.' He said the recommendation to mercy would be forwarded to the proper quarter be he 'must build no hope upon it.' However, it appears the luck of the devil was with Poulter and his sentence was commuted.

16 JANUARY 1857

Reported case of garrotters at Cambridge. Four men who gave their names as John Johnson, James Miller, John Smith and ? Williams, all of them strangers in the town, were brought before the Borough Police Court. Jonathan Ambery, an undergraduate at St John's College, stated, 'When I came within about 10yds of St Edwards passage I felt and saw an arm put round my throat. I saw no one; my assailants were behind me; I heard the voices of two. I was choked and drawn backwards until I lost my equilibrium.' He was then 'dashed with violence on to the ground' where the unfortunate young man's head smashed against the pavement and he was rendered insensible. His assailants then proceeded to go through his pockets, stealing his watch, a papier-mâché snuff box, a gold pin and about 2*d* in coppers. The assault was committed just below the window of the Three Tuns pub; someone threw up a window and called out. Mr Scott, an under-porter at Jesus College, came to Ambery's aid and was instrumental in the apprehension of the assailant, who gave his name as John Johnson. All four garrotters were remanded in custody.

17 JANUARY Strange Tales and Folklore of Cambridgeshire: Freeing the Bride

In Bluntisham the old country rite of debt freeing is recorded. Any bride in debt before her marriage could free herself from such fiscal embarrassment by walking across the road naked to her future husband's house, thus leaving her past behind and placing herself totally in his care.

18 JANUARY 1911

The Ramsey Arson Case concludes at Huntingdon Assizes. Walter Beeby, a groom, had been charged with causing four fires on the farm of Mr J.I. Major at Ramsey, where his father was farm foreman, on 23 and 24 October 1910. The first fire had been attributed to a chaff cutter overheating, but George Desborough, who had been in charge of the machine, deposed it could not have done so without his knowledge. Inspector Storey said that after the first fire he told Beeby that Mr Major had suspicions that someone had set fire to the stacks – Beeby replied that he did not do it. Storey charged Beeby on suspicion but because he could not obtain a cart, Storey allowed his prisoner to ride with him towards Ramsey on a bicycle. However, the good Inspector's trust was misplaced and as they rode along Beeby suddenly took off down another road and got clear away. Later found and brought into custody, Beeby gave a statement in which he attempted to give himself an alibi for when the fires started. The jury remained unconvinced and found him guilty. Beeby was sentenced to five years' penal servitude.

19 JANUARY 1847

Fatal railway accident at Whittlesford. The two daughters of farmer Collman of Duckworth, both in their twenties, went to Whittlesford railway station to see a friend off to Saffron Walden. The train was late, but the sisters eventually saw the lady off and then jumped down onto the permanent way to get to the other platform, where the gate was situated for their homeward journey. At this instant the 6 p.m. evening express from London was steaming towards the station, travelling at at least 30–35mph. Mr Jackson, the station master, and a porter shouted warnings, the porter managing to pull one of the women back, undoubtedly saving her life. The other sister met an instant death. The engine was unable to stop for another 400yds. Upon a search of the area, one of the porters found a bonnet; upon lifting it, the head of the poor girl fell out. A few yards further up the line was found the trunk of her body, one of the severed arms and part of the right leg. As many body parts as could be found were gathered together and taken to the Red Lion Inn. An inquest held later, and a verdict of 'Accidental Death' was recorded.

20 JANUARY 1606 (in the modern calendar this is 30 January 1607)

Extensive flooding across southern Britain. A contemporary pamphlet stated:

> These towns and villages were overflowed, that is to say Wisbech, Guyhorn, Parson Drove and Hobshouse. This Hobshouse being an almes house [and the water having broken down the walls of said building] the winds blew the clothes off from the bed of a poore man and his wife; they being cold waked and sodainly stept up to the belly in water and then he thinking himself to be in danger and he knowing the best way to escape the danger of the water, took his wife on his necke and carried her away and so both were saved.

21 JANUARY Tales from the Gaols: Broad Arrow Men

A familiar term for prisoners in the late nineteenth and early twentieth centuries was 'Broad Arrow Men', an epithet gained from the distinctive broad arrow or 'crow's foot' stamped onto all prison uniforms. The origins of the symbol date back to the seventeenth century, when a Master of the Ordnances in the Tower of London began marking the weaponry as Tower property with an arrow-like device from his coat of arms. Over the years this symbol has been adopted by all government departments to denote equipment from rifles to rulers as Government Issue. The broad arrow was stamped onto prison garb not only to create a 'dress of shame' to be worn by convicts but to make the clothes they wore so distinctive they would stand out as a convict if they affected an escape. Broad Arrows were discontinued on prison uniforms in 1922.

22 JANUARY 1690

Sent down. In 1690 Dr John Peachell, Master of Magdalene College, starved himself to death. Archbishop Sancroft had rebuked Dr Peachell for setting an ill example in the university by drunkenness and other loose conduct. His penance was four days' abstinence after which he would have eaten, but could not.

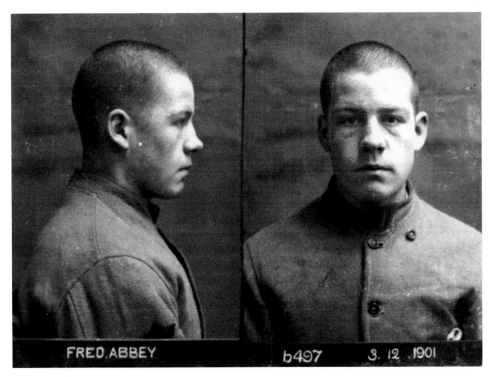

Young convict Frederick Abbey – a 'Broad Arrow Man'.

23 JANUARY 1876

A shocking scene occurred at Ely workhouse. A butcher named Henry Briggs, who was awaiting removal to a lunatic asylum, seized a red-hot poker from the fire and thrust it several times into his body. He then rushed at the attendants, who fled, one of them dropping a pocketknife with which the maniac cut his own throat from ear to ear. He died of his injuries the following day.

24 JANUARY Cures of Fenland Cunning Folk: The Wonders of Dung

Early morning dew on a cow pat was seen as a particularly efficacious cure for spots and blemishes. Put your finger in the moisture, dab it on your acne and it was said to soon clear up. The healing powers of dung dew were said to have remarkable qualities – take one spoon of it a day and you would be cured of tuberculosis.

If you were suffering from chilblains a cure oft suggested well into the twentieth century was to hop out into the field, find a nice fresh cow pat and put your foot in it.

Dung and the 'healing herbs within it', when mingled with honey and warmed over a slow fire and applied as a poultice, was also said to cure persistent boils and breast abcess. Startle a cow and make it drop its dung – this was said to make a fine poultice to blanch freckles and the marks of ringworm. A dung poultice was even used as a cure for babies' cradle cap. Chicken or goose dung regularly massaged into the scalp was also considered an effective cure for baldness.

25 JANUARY 1936

The Revd Barnard Halsey Tyrwhitt-Drake (52), rector of Walsoken, was killed by a falling tree. Alfred Freeman had told the rector to keep well out of the way as he felled the tree. It was dark and, worryingly, when Freeman went to look for the rector he could not find him. After a search the unfortunate vicar was found lying face downwards with his head buried about 5–6in in the ground. He had been struck by a branch of the tree as it fell and his neck was found to have been broken.

26 JANUARY Punishments of the Past: The Stocks and Whipping Post

The stocks are probably the oldest and most widely used punitive device for punishment of minor offenders such as beggars, drunkards, louts, prostitutes and scolds. The absence of stocks and a whipping post in a village after 1405 would downgrade the status of a village to a mere hamlet. Widely used up to the early nineteenth century, an order for new stocks for 'setting and placing drunken and disorderly persons therein' in the parishes of Cambridge was made as late as June 1785. Whipping was a punishment

The village stocks and whipping post under the old chestnut tree at Meldreth.

used for a variety of crimes, often against those who had had a few sittings in the stocks but appeared not to have repented their ways. There are many instances of women being whipped for whoring and men and women being 'whipped for a rogue'. The constable's accounts for the parish of Great Staughton in 1680 state 'Paid 8s 6d in charges for taking up a distracted woman, watching her and whipping her the next day.' Another account from 1710 states how Nurse London was paid 2s for searching a woman to check she was not 'with child' before she was whipped. In the same year Thomas Hawkins was paid 8d for whipping two people that had smallpox. One of the last public whippings recorded in Huntingdonshire took place at St Ives in July 1788, when John Shickles suffered the punishment after stealing several articles of wearing apparel from a lighter cabin – after which he was also given six months in the House of Correction. Examples of stocks still on display in Cambridgeshire villages include Elton, Burwell and Meldreth.

27 JANUARY 1838

A report was published in the *Cambridge Chronicle* of a fight that had erupted between a Littleport overseer and a local butcher. These two upstanding gentlemen exchanged blows for well over an hour and a half while, as the report went on to point out, two local constables 'either insensible of their duty as peace officers, or enjoying the disgraceful scene, allowed the peace of the town to be disturbed.'

28 JANUARY 1836

One for the cage! Chatteris farm labourer Will Palmer (18) was known for his alcohol-fuelled violence. On 28 January he was in his cups again sloughing along the village street when he encountered elderly Mr Briggs, who was blind. For no apparent reason Palmer hit the old man across the face. A boy of 10 ran over to intervene; Palmer lashed out at the boy. The lad fetched the constable and found John Palmer (no relation) on duty. He rushed to the scene and tried to reason with Palmer and asked him to go home quietly. Palmer the rogue was having none of it and despite the constable giving him a stern warning and even taking him by the arm and attempting to lead him to his own house, Palmer persisted. Constable Palmer then began to drag the miscreant to the village lock-up; Palmer fought, so the constable forced him to sit in a wheelbarrow, to which he was then tied and pushed to 'the cage'. As the constable attempted to manacle the prisoner, Palmer kept kicking, beating and even biting the constable. Palmer made no defence at his trial.

On enquiry with the gaoler, it appeared Palmer had been a regular visitor held under summary convictions for assaults and that he had only been discharged a week previous to the assault after serving two months for beating his father. The judge handed down six months' imprisonment with hard labour and hoped that would make some impression upon Palmer.

29 JANUARY Grim Sayings of Cambridgeshire: Fen Folk Occupations

The following is a poem describing the occupations of Fen folk, published in *Polyolbion* (1662):

The Toyling fisher here is Tweing of his net,
The fowler is imployed his lymed twigs to set.
One underneath his horse to get a shoote doth stalk,

Another over dykes upon his stilts doth walk.
There others with their spades the peats are squaring out
And others from their Carres are busily about
To draw out sedge and reed for thatch and stover fit.

30 JANUARY 1844

A fire was discovered in a farm tenanted by Mr Smith near the centre of the village of Colne near Somersham. High winds fanned the flames and within minutes the farm and a number of adjoining barns, farm buildings and properties were ablaze. Ephraim Raper was one of the first on the scene, only to be horrified to observe his own barn on fire at the extreme end of the village. A third house soon caught fire and it was observed that three distinct fires were soon blazing at such a distance apart 'they had the least communication with the other.' Numerous houses were 'reduced to ashes' including the Ship pub. The local press was left in no doubt these were deliberate fires started by an incendiary or arsonist (it turned out to be a disgruntled farm labourer from nearby Bluntisham).

31 JANUARY 1924

Escaped Prisoner. Thomas Stead (a.k.a. George Harrison, Thomas McKin and T. Curtis) after his initial hearing at Peterborough was being handed over by his police escort at the gate of Leicester Gaol when he made a sudden dash and escaped into the darkness. Formerly an engraver and designer at the Norwich School of Art, Stead had established himself aboard a derelict submarine chaser on the River Yare near Norwich, where he had a printing press and forger's plant printing £1 Bank of England notes. His description was circulated and a reward of £10 was offered for his capture. Stead's run gained him a total of four months' freedom, but he was eventually recaptured, tried and found guilty at Peterborough Quarter Sessions and sentenced to five years' penal servitude.

FEBRUARY

On 1 February 1870 newspapers reported a near fatality at the grand skating match for the Championship of the Fens held on Welney Wash, Bedford Level. In front of 5,000 spectators, sixteen of the best Fen skaters competed in some good races, but there had been a rapid thaw. Mr Fletcher of Soham Fen fell while racing with 'Turkey' Smart. Being a heavy man and falling with great force, the ice broke and he was immediately immersed. The crowd was horrified, but he was extracted alive, albeit with great difficulty, using ropes. Rescue achieved, the championship continued and was won by young Mr Hills of Welney.

1 FEBRUARY 1913

Two bodies were discovered in the tea room of the Temperance Hotel, St Ives. Identified as Gustave Kunne (44) and Elizabeth Warnes, the hotel proprietor, both had been stabbed through the heart. Warnes had separated from her husband, after increasingly violent rows, in 1909. After her separation Mrs Warnes had taken on the Temperance Hotel and had become friendly with Kunne soon after his arrival in the town. The bodies had been found with Kunne lying on his left side over the waist of Mrs Warnes, a bloodstained Norwegian fishing knife, known to be similar to one carried by Kunne, was found nearby. Curiously a lamp had been knocked over, the glass broken and paraffin spilt, but it had been stood up again on a nearby table; there was no other sign of a struggle. At the inquest, Dr Groves, who had been called to the scene and conducted the post-mortem, did not believe there was any third party involved and concluded Kunne killed Warnes then turned the blade on himself immediately afterwards. The evidence was not clear cut but the coroner, clearly tiring of the enquiry, simplified the options for the jury, asking them to consider if the woman killed the man, vice versa, or did they commit suicide? The jury returned a verdict of 'murder and *felo de se*' – Kunne murdered Warnes then committed suicide.

2 FEBRUARY 1799

Heavy snow had fallen but Elizabeth Woodcock of Impington valiantly managed to wade her way through to Cambridge Saturday Market, where she sold her eggs and butter. After replenishing her flask with brandy at the Three Tuns on Castle Hill she set off home. Just outside Impington she was thrown from her horse and being shaken by the fall and, numbed by the freezing cold, she was unable to remount (although some accounts stated she was in fact too drunk to remount). Elizabeth took shelter under a hedge, the snow began to drift and soon she was completely entombed. As hours and days passed she heard the church bells and the voices of people in the distance. On the Monday she summoned enough energy to tie her red handkerchief to a stick and pushed it up through a gap in the snow. This makeshift flag did lead to her discovery – but not until a week later! William Munsey, the Parish Clerk of Impington, spotted the 'flag', discovered the frozen Elizabeth, and summoned help. Mrs Woodcock had spent eight days buried in the snow and lived to tell the tale – but not for long; she was taken ill and died on 24 July, aged 43.

3 FEBRUARY 1852

A State of Public Health report stated:

> In the sub-district of Soham, in Cambridgeshire, the deaths, which had been 50 in the corresponding quarter of 1852, rose to 112 last quarter, in consequence of cholera in October and November, which was fatal to 61 persons. In the district of Ely, in the same county, a great deal of fever prevailed at Stretham, and 2 cases of cholera occurred at Haddenham, while in the parish of Sutton diarrhoea attacked the inmates of almost every house. The deaths were 61 in the sub-district of Ely, against 39 in the corresponding quarter of 1852, and 17 of those were caused by cholera.

Elizabeth Woodcock of Impington, entombed in snow, 1799.

4 FEBRUARY John Howard Reports on the Prisons of Cambridgeshire & Huntingdon

Cambridge Castle ,1782. Gaoler Simon Saunders.

The prison is the gate of the old castle. On the ground floor, called the low-gaol are three strong rooms, one for male felons (30ft by 6ft 7ins); another for women (16ft by 9) with a chimney: the other was not finished. There is an ascent of 22 stone steps on the outside to the debtors' apartments, called the high-gaol. On the first floor is a room for the turnkey, a large kitchen and two or three other rooms. Above them are five rooms and a condemned room. All the rooms are sizeable. Clauses of act against spirituous liquors hung up, by a written order of Thomas Cockran Esq., Sheriff. The act for preserving health of prisoners not hung up. Straw 20s a year. The castle yard is spacious but not safe and prisoners have not the use of it. In it is the gallows.

Debtors have some relief from legacies and donations paid by several colleges: from Sidney College, each has a shirt every year and a sack of coals. From St John's sixteen pennyworth of bread every Sunday morning. A collection is made in the university and town by leave of the Mayor, which amounts to about £7 a year. Twenty shillings, deducting land tax, was also paid from an estate at Croxton.

5 FEBRUARY 1832

It was reported that an Irish tramp was committed to Peterborough gaol for a savage and deadly attack on a soldier from a recruiting party. The two had met in the kitchen of the Golden Lion pub when there was an altercation between them. The tramp exited but waited outside for the soldier to leave and, when he did, set about him with a large knife. The cuts rained down on the soldier's face and head; having mauled him to the ground the tramp left the knife sticking firmly in the soldier's skull. The report concluded 'there are now, however, hopes of his recovery.'

6 FEBRUARY

Wandlebury Ring. Wandlebury Ring is an Iron-Age hill fort dating back 2,500 years. A legend attached to it recorded in *Otia Imperialia* by Gervase of Tilbury in the early twelfth century tells how, if a knight dared to enter it by moonlight and cried 'Knight to knight, come forth', a ghostly night-rider would appear and do battle. One such knight was Sir Osbert, who was met by the Black Knight by moonlight. After a fierce exchange, Sir Osbert gained an advantage and knocked the night-rider to the ground. As victor of

Sir Osbert, the victor of the combat with the Black Knight of Wandlebury Ring.

the contest, Osbert claimed his adversary's steed. The infuriated night-rider threw his lance at Osbert and disappeared. The weapon only caught him a glancing cut to the thigh and was quick to heal but every anniversary of his fight with the night-rider the wound would open up again as if fresh, bleed profusely, and then heal again immediately.

7 FEBRUARY 1823

The *Cambridge Chronicle* carries news of the arrest of notorious Littleport poacher John Rolfe. It was not his illicit hunt for game that brought him in this time but the cold-blooded murder of William Landon, his friend and poaching companion, at Plantation Farm, Burnt Fen. Tried and found guilty, Rolfe was hanged on the Ely gallows before a crowd of 5,000 on 24 February 1823. His body was later encased in a gibbet cage and suspended from a 24ft-high gibbet erected upon Padnal Fen.

8 FEBRUARY 1895

The inquest opened into the death of Thomas Hensman of Kimbolton. Dr Hallett had discovered the unfortunate gentleman quaking with cold and covered by old coats. Hallett had attempted to restore Hensman, but he 'sank and died'. Hensman had lived in a large house by himself with plenty of coals, silver plate and good furniture. He was also found to have been given financial assistance by friends, but he chose not to use it. The jury found he had died from lack of food, clothing and warmth – the result of self neglect.

9 FEBRUARY 1927

An inquest was held at Cambridge Coroner's Court upon the body of James Handley Seymour, an undergraduate who had been found dead in his garage. PC Holmes described how Seymour's head had been found 'right down in the engine of the car.' The scarf the young man had been wearing had become entangled and wound around the magneto, strangling him so tightly that it had to be cut through to get the body away from the car. A verdict of 'accidental death from asphyxiation' was recorded.

10 FEBRUARY 1795

After a season of deep snow and frost, the thaw causes flooding. The bridge was carried away at Barton Mills and water ran over the high walks at King's College and St John's in Cambridge. The road at the back of the colleges was for some hours impassable and mail coaches could not get through from the county. A valiant man with a cart plied a watery route from opposite Magdalene College to the great bridge. Another enterprising fellow was the Guard from the St Ives Mail Coach who, determined to get the post through, hired a boat to carry both mail and man to Fen Stanton.

11 FEBRUARY 1839

Mr Kenyon, gamekeeper to the Earl of Hardwicke, and a number of his men were watching part of the game preserve at Wimpole, known as the Reed Pond Pightle. The keepers heard feet splashing in the water of the pond, and, hiding to observe who was making the noise, they saw a group of poachers coming out of the gloom, one of them with a gun. Kenyon gave a signal, but hearing this the poachers fled. One of the poachers, James Lyon, was looking over his shoulder as he ran; Keeper Rooke stepped out from behind a tree and Lyon ran into his arms. Brought before the assizes, the judge was pleased to learn Lyon's 'offered no violence' at the time of his capture and said he was being lenient as he handed down six months' imprisonment.

12 FEBRUARY Cures of Fenland Cunning Folk: Opium

For centuries the Fen folk were plagued with ailments such as malaria, rheumatism, asthma and ague. A universal 'cure all' was to drink or eat the seed of the great white poppies – opium. Some labourers frequently took poppy head tea for their meal breaks, probably to relieve the daily drudge. This potent brew was used to delay the onset of labour by mixing it with gin, and it was even used as a tincture to quiet and sooth teething children! As the old couplet stated:

> Poppy Tea and Opium pill
> Are the Fen cure for many an ill.

Opium eating remained a common habit across the Fens well into the nineteenth century, indeed the practice extended to the Isle of Ely, south to St Ives and in the west as far as Whittlesea. Some addicts, men and women, were known to take between forty and ninety grains a day (about thirty grains could be bought for a penny). A reporter from the *Morning Chronicle* stated: 'the sale of laudanum in Ely was as common as the sale of butter and cheese.' The article went so far as to dub Ely 'the opium eating city'.

13 FEBRUARY 1891

Mrs Anne Mason (68) of Cambridge Street, Godmanchester was in her scullery when her husband Sam (76) entered and proceeded to attack her with a cricket bat, leaving her in a pool of blood. He then left the house and walked down the street to the Hog and Chequers pub. Anne managed to drag herself out of the house towards the Swan pub opposite, where she raised the alarm. When the police arrived at the Hog and Chequers the old man resignedly asked, 'I suppose you want me?' as they entered. He was originally charged with aggravated assault, however, after Anne died, the charge was altered to one of 'wilful murder'. Brought to trial, the old man was declared insane and detained in an asylum for the rest of his life.

14 FEBRUARY 1840

Infant Jane Rumbold dies at her family home in Bassingbourn-cum-Kneesworth. Born the previous December, she had been baptised by the local non-conformist minister, but when the grieving family applied to the local vicar to bury Jane in the parish churchyard Revd W.H. Chapman refused permission. They tried bringing their funeral cortège to the churchyard, not just once but five times, but still the cleric would not relent – he refused to bury any child baptised at the non-conformist meeting. The case was taken to the High Court, and as the legal process was pursued, the child's coffin was kept in a recess in an empty chimney. When baptism was declared valid the obstinate rector still refused to carry out the committal and it was the W. Coulcher of nearby Whaddon who eventually conducted the burial on a bitterly cold 30 January 1845, five years after her death.

15 FEBRUARY Tales from the Gaols: The Separate and Silent System

During the nineteenth century, the 'Separate and Silent System' was introduced so that every prisoner, once admitted to gaol, would be kept in solitary confinement and maintain silence to all apart from prison officers and officials when addressed. In the exercise yard male prisoners would wear masks, which would only allow the prisoner to see the ground, and women wore veils so no prisoner could recognise one another. Prisoners were exercised in groups with long lengths of chain that was not allowed to touch the ground to ensure they kept their distance and did not communicate. Prisoners were not allowed visitors. They were to be reformed through solitude to contemplate their wrongs, prayer, work and religious instruction. Even prison chapels had stalls rather than pews for the inmates. The prison chaplain would look out on a congregation in what appeared to be upright coffins!

Prisoners taking exercise. Their bonnets or masks blinker their eyes so that they can only see the floor and each man holds a knot in the rope to space him from the man in front.

16 FEBRUARY Punishments of the Past: The Pillory

The Pillory was an effective and humiliating punishment for fraud, perjury, seditious speech and sexual crimes, and its use can be traced back to the statutes of the thirteenth century. In England, pillories were considered so essential by the authorities that towns risked forfeiting the right to hold a market by not having one. Here the miscreant would be seen by all and could well be pelted with rotten fruit and vegetables, mud, excrement and even dead animals to varying degrees depending on the crime the culprit committed and the mood of the crowd. The last man pilloried in England was Peter Bossy for lying under oath. His punishment was carried out on Tower Hill, London on 22 June 1832.

*An unfortunate man suffering
a 'stand' in the pillory during
the seventeenth century.*

17 FEBRUARY 1855

On this day Wilkinson Crowe, who had been skating towards Ely from Littleport, fell
through the ice and was drowned.

18 FEBRUARY Cures of Fenland Cunning Folk: Hedgehogs

Cures obtained from gypsies were considered particularly potent; a number of these
were based around hedgehogs. Gypsies ate hedgehogs after baking them in mud casings
– when the mud was peeled away the spines went with it, leaving just the cooked meat.
New mothers were often prescribed this food as it was believed to enrich their blood after
child birth; the same food was offered as a treatment for those suffering with anaemia.

19 FEBRUARY 1848

Reports were published of the inquest at the Anchor, Littleport, upon Elizabeth Crabb,
'a quiet inoffensive woman who never did nobody no harm.' Her relationship with her

husband, John Crabb, was far from harmonious and the evidence of the animosity he had shown her over the years led the jury to return a verdict of 'wilful murder' against him. Brought before the Cambridgeshire Assizes the following March, the jury found Crabb guilty of manslaughter and he was sentenced to two years' hard labour.

20 FEBRUARY Cures of Fenland Cunning Folk: Charming Warts

A popular method of getting rid of warts in the Fens was to rub them with a raw potato at midnight. When in season the inside of a broad bean pod could also be rubbed on the wart. Another 'cure' suggests rubbing the wart with a piece of meat, especially liver – bury the meat in the garden then, as it decomposes, the wart does likewise.

Alternatively, each wart should be touched by the sufferer with a piece of straw. The sufferer should then close their eyes and throw the straw over their left shoulder. Yet another method was to tie horse hair round the warts then anoint each one with seven drops of blood from the snout of a freshly killed mole.

If the wart or warts persisted, a professional charmer may well be consulted. Some patients would 'sell' their wart to a wart buyer. Alternatively, after crossing the palm of the charmer with a copper coin, the advice imparted would be 'to count the warts then take a black snail and stick it on a thorn bush'; as the snail perishes, the blemishes would disappear – provided the sufferer did not tell a soul of their actions in this process.

21 FEBRUARY 1742

Murder victim Elizabeth Pateman (18), a servant, was buried at Steeple Morden. The perpetrators were never brought to justice, but the story attached to this crime from 'local knowledge' handed down the generations is that Pateman had either witnessed the murder or the disposal of the body of a packman or pedlar who had come to her master's house at Moco Farm. She was overheard telling her sweetheart of 'a secret', so the farmer and his wife killed the girl to ensure her silence. Upon her tombstone were carved the implements said to have been used to kill her – a pea hook, a knife and a coulter.

22 FEBRUARY 1931

Between the hours of 11 p.m. and midnight Mr Frederick John Charles Ellis, a first-year student, died in his room at Sidney Sussex College. His body was discovered at 7 a.m. the following morning lying fully clothed on the floor; his hands were found tied together behind his back with handkerchiefs and khaki puttees and his arms secured by electric flex. Further handkerchiefs were tied over his mouth and nostrils, all of them knotted in a methodical and neat fashion. His head was pushed into a thick cushion. The Cambridge Borough Police alerted Scotland Yard and Chief Inspector Helby and Detective Sergeant Bell were sent poste haste with pathologist Sir Bernard Spilsbury. The key question for Spilsbury and the investigating officers was if it had been possible for Ellis to tie himself up, or had Ellis had been killed by accident during some student prank?

Members of the Pentacle Club, the University Magician's Society, were interrogated. Further enquires revealed Ellis had been involved in a 'craze' which had lasted for a couple of terms involving experiments and competitions in binding one another with ropes and handkerchiefs to see who could be the first to free themselves. At the inquest, Spilsbury testified that in his opinion 'nobody else was responsible for the tying up' and 'there was no indication of anyone else having been in the room.' The jury retired for an hour before returning a verdict of 'death by asphyxia due to an accident', the foreman adding they did not consider that any blame should be attached to the college authorities.

23 FEBRUARY 1666

Plague rages in Ramsey. A local story tells of how Colonel William Cromwell, cousin of the Lord Protector, brought the plague to the town by ordering a bolt of cloth to be sent from London which he wanted to have made into a coat. Whatever the truth may be, Colonel Cromwell died and soon the tailor, all his family, and around 400 people from Ramsey all succumbed to the pestilence.

24 FEBRUARY 1888

Fatal accident at Cambridge boat races. The Clare boat had bumped Queen's at First Post Corner, and were drawing to the bank, then Trinity Hall came up, hotly pursued by Emmanuel, who had made their bump. The Trinity boat ran over the iron riggers into the Clare boat, and the prow of it penetrated the chest of Mr E.S. Campbell of the Clare College crew, literally lifting him off his seat. He received the blow over the region of the heart between two ribs, and died within a few minutes.

25 FEBRUARY Grim Tales of Cambridgeshire: The Fen Tigers

True Fen men, proudly known as Fen Tigers, had a fearsome reputation for defending their way of life and working lands. In 1630 Charles I asked the Earl of Bedford to undertake the drainage of the Fens. Bedford and thirteen other 'Adventurers' employed the experienced Dutch engineer Cornelius Vermuyden to direct the works. The original plan was to cut a number of new drains, the greatest being what is now known as the 'Old Bedford River' that stretches 21 miles from Earith to Salter's Lode. The Fen Tigers saw this as not only a threat to their way of life but also an unwanted intrusion by outsiders. Riots and disturbances broke out and the embankments and sluices erected by the workmen by day were soon destroyed overnight. Workmen were intimidated with threats of violence; several of those who chose to call the bluff of the Fen Tigers were attacked, some killed and their bodies found left as a warning to others – many more are undoubtedly still residing in makeshift and watery graves under the Fens.

26 FEBRUARY 1930

Eileen Allen Woolfe (39), proprietor of River Cottage and Dance Room, Fen Ditton, was brought before Bottisham Police Court charged with knowingly allowing the premises to be used for immoral purposes. Her son, Peter, also stood charged with aiding and abetting. The prosecution alleged 'that women of known undesirable character had been seen to resort to the premises with men, mostly members of the University.' While under police observation, women were seen to come and go with men wearing caps and gowns. The Chief Proctor of the University went to investigate. By the light of his lamp he could see four men who appeared to be undergraduates and seven girls, both of the accused and an elderly man. The Proctor asked the men if they were members of the university – they admitted they were and he ordered them back to their colleges. The cases were adjourned.

27 FEBRUARY Punishments of the Past: The Birch and the Lash

The birch was reserved mostly as a corporal punishment for wayward boys found guilty of petty offences. Cambridgeshire Constabulary Orders from the early twentieth century stated:

> Owing to the difference in age, nervous temperament and physical constitution, punishment must necessarily vary. The birching of children under 10 years should be less severe than in the case of older offenders. Birching to be administered by a Police Constable in the presence of an officer not below the rank of Inspector. Parents are to be invited to attend.

Adult males found guilty of crimes against the person, such as robbery with violence, could be sentenced to receive 'the lash', also known as flogging – this punishment could

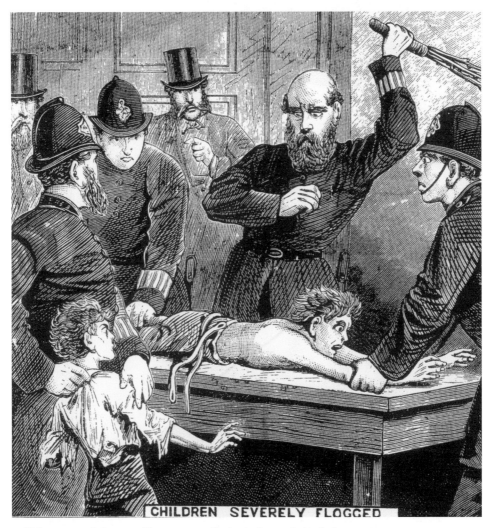

CHILDREN SEVERELY FLOGGED

Held down securely by constables, a young offender is about to be birched.

The Caxton Gibbet.

also be used on criminals who seriously transgress prison rules by, for example, assaulting a prison officer; just such an incident and punishment took place at the Cambridge Gaol as late as 1904 after a prisoner attacked Warder Andrews with a hatchet.

28 FEBRUARY 1863

The Comberton Witchcraft case. An inquest was held on the body of Emma Rust (18), a poor girl who had died after suffering a succession of violent fits. Testimony was given that it was believed the girl had been bewitched and, rather than call for a doctor, the villagers had sent for Mother Stonebridge of Potton to 'deliver' Emma from witchcraft. The inquest returned a verdict of 'death by natural causes', but not without a stern rebuke to the villagers for not seeking medical advice and thereby causing the expense of an inquest!

29 FEBRUARY Grim Tales of Cambridgeshire: The Caxton Gibbet

The Caxton Gibbet, as described in the eighteenth century, was set upon a small knoll beside the ancient Ermine Street (now the A1198). The upright and crossbeam we see today is a relatively modern reproduction made with old timbers. An account believed to relate to Caxton Gibbet written by Cambridgeshire antiquarian William Cole (1714–1782) states:

> About 1753 or 1754 the son of Mrs Gatward being convicted of robbing the Mail was hanged in chains on the Great Road. I saw him hanging in a scarlet coat after he had hung 2 or 4 months it is supposed that the screw was filed which supported him and that he fell in the first high wind after. Mr Lord of Trinity, passed by as he lay on the ground, and, trying to open his breast, to see what state his body was in, not being offensive, but quite dry.

MARCH

The headstone of William Simonds, who died at Woodditton on 1 March 1757 aged 80.
Behind the grill at the top of the stone is his iron dish or drippin pan. The inscription reads:

Here lies my corpse, who was the man,
That lov'd a sop in dripping pan.
But now believe me I am dead,
Now here the pan stands at my head.
Still for sop to the last I cry'd,
But could not eat and so I died.
My neighbours they perhaps may laugh,
Now they do read my epitaph.

1 MARCH 1905

The King of the Hoaxers. Cambridge was preparing for a visit by the Sultan of Zanzibar. Notification had been sent by telegram to the mayor stating the Sultan and his retinue would be arriving from King's Cross by midday on 2 March and would be glad if the mayor would give them lunch and show them around Cambridge during the course of the afternoon. The program was duly carried out and the Sultan expressed himself pleased with the reception. It later transpired the whole visit had been a costumed hoax perpetrated by Horace De Vere Cole, a third year undergraduate at Trinity. On another occasion, Cole bet a Member of Parliament that he couldn't beat him to the nearest corner, even with a 10yds head start. Having already slipped his gold watch into the MP's pocket, as the MP began to run, Cole summoned the police who promptly arrested the 'pickpocket' and took him to the nearest police station. However, Cole's HMS *Dreadnought* hoax in 1910 was his finest. Cole sent a telegram purportedly from Foreign Office Under-Secretary Sir Charles Hardinge to HMS *Dreadnought*, informing the captain that he should prepare for an official visit from a group of princes from Abyssinia. A group of students then inspected the ship and presented cards printed in Swahili, talking to each other in a broken Latin. To show their appreciation, they exclaimed invented phrases such as 'bunga-bunga' and even bestowed fake military honours on some of the officers. They got away with it despite one of them sneezing and blowing off his false whiskers; luckily he managed to stick them back on before anyone noticed.

2 MARCH 1861

Augustus Hilton (23), corn miller, had returned home to Parson Drove from Wisbech Market with his wife at about 4 p.m. They had argued over money; Hilton claimed his wife had not given him enough to pay for some wheat. The dispute continued over tea. Hilton asked his wife to pour him another cup, but she replied, 'No, you've been slandering me all the time I was at Wisbech, and do you think I come home to wait on you in this way? No, I won't; I'll die first.' He replied, 'So you shall.' A short while later she was discovered upstairs with her throat cut, she died about twenty minutes later. Mr Hilton proceeded to his father's house where he sat by the fire smoking and drinking brandy and water until the constable came to arrest him. While in custody he enquired, 'When shall I be hanged? I want to die. I want to go to my wife.'

At the Cambridge Assizes Hilton pleaded 'guilty'. Mr Justice Wightman explained to Hilton the grave consequences his plea would incur and asked if he wished to reconsider, to which Hilton replied, 'I won't alter it.' Hilton was hanged upon the Cambridge gallows on 10 August 1861. A witness recorded:

> When he reached the summit of the scaffold, 'he made one hurried glance at the thousands of assembled round the hill and hung down his head as if deeply affected. The cap was shortly placed over his face by Calcraft, and as the clergyman was saying 'In the midst of life we are in death,' the bolt was withdrawn, and the hapless man ceased to exist in a very brief period.

3 MARCH 1844

Wicken labourer James Peachey was drinking at the Prince Albert in Soham with his friends Robert and David Bayley; Henry Hills (20) and his pal Will Steadman were also there. Peachey and his friends left first and claimed that for no apparent reason Henry Hills caught up with their group, struck down Peachey, and walked on. Peachey claimed that Hills and Steadman had gone off with his hat and they managed to get to the home of Hills' father and bolted the door. When Peachey and the Bayleys brothers arrived, Mr Hills got his sons and threw the boys off the premises. They soon returned again, but this time the younger Hills met them armed with a bludgeon and dealt Peachey such a blow it 'wholly unsensed him'. Or at least that was what he told the constable.

At the assizes a completely different tale was told by the Hills family, Will Steadman and his father Robert. They claimed they had passed the boys on the street and one of the Bayleys had threatened to give Robert Steadman 'a good hiding'. Pursued to the Hills' house, the Bayleys set to with Will Stedman and a battle royal of six rounds commenced between Peachey and Robert Steadman. Peachey was floored by a blow which knocked him insensible and required a doctor. Steadman denied he used any bludgeon on Peachey. It was up to the jury to decide who was speaking the truth; they believed the Hills and Steadman families and Henry Hills walked free.

4 MARCH Strange Tales and Folklore of Cambridgeshire: The Witchbone

Ploughmen, horse tamers, bull handlers, horse doctors and snake catchers would have had a Witchbone to 'charm' the creatures which were key to their occupations. Up until the early twentieth century a 'sacred' belief was placed in the secret of the Witchbone (also known as the Witch Stone, Toad Stone or Toad Bone). Tom Money, head horse keeper at Spinney Abbey, recalled:

> If you want to make a witchbone take a walking toad, a natterjack, and bury him at midnight in an ant heap. That's what Mark Thorby used to do, he could tame any hoss that ever wass. He'd go to that ant heap every night at midnight to see how the ants were getting on with the job. When they'd cleaned every mite of flesh off the bones, he's pick them bones up and go down at midnight to the Runawater, the only fast running stream in the parish, and hull 'em into the water. The bone that floated furthest upstream, again the current, was the witchbone. So Mark grabbed that right smart. He allus kept it in his pocket.

The toad featured in much fen lore and medicine.

5 MARCH 1913

Swavesey makes the front page of the *Daily Mirror* after fire swept through the village, leaving more than sixty-three people without a home, among them eight widows of more than 70 years of age. The fire had broken out on Taylors Lane on the afternoon of 3 March after a spark from a cottage chimney set light to thatch. Despite the rapid attendance by the local fire brigade, it proved difficult to obtain water from the public supply and the wind caused the fire to spread rapidly. The St Ives fire brigade arrived by late afternoon with two horse-drawn manual pumps, and a steam fire engine arrived from Huntingdon by early evening, but they could do nothing to control the blaze and ended up just damping down the smouldering ruins of twenty-eight cottages and numerous outbuildings.

6 MARCH 1823

Robert Head was executed on this day upon the Ely gallows for burglary.

7 MARCH 1791

Bartholomew Quailn executed at Kennington Common. Quailn, a 'poor labourer', lived with his family in the Isle of Ely. Quailn, with his infant child on one arm, and a coarse bag on the other, had followed his wife Ann out of their local pub; he was drunk, she was not. An argument arose between the two and he threw her to the ground and violently kicked her several times. She clawed herself up but he threw her down again and gave her several more kicks, upon which she clapped her hand to her side and was heard to exclaim, 'Oh, Bat, now you have done for me!' She died soon after. Sobered by his actions, Quailn immediately showed great grief and concern for her death. The post-mortem revealed Mrs Quailn's spleen had been burst by the kicks. The judge's quandary over whether Quailn had murdered his wife or whether her death was occasioned only after 'reasonable chastisement' led to the decision being passing from the Ely Assizes to the King's Bench in London. The bench pronounced that the kicking was a deliberate act; from which, as death ensued, it was adjudged to be murder. Sentence of death was passed with the provision Quailn's body be delivered to the surgeons to be dissected and anatomised.

8 MARCH 1833

William Davis, William Douse and Thomas Evitt were brought before the assizes for burglary at the home of Mr Barber of Great Stukeley. It was pointed out that the previous incumbent of the house in question had been the Revd Waterhouse who had been murdered by Joshua Slade in 1827. On the 3 August Mr Barber left to attend a dinner party. Upon his return the following morning he found his pear tree near the house had been cut away and the lattice work pulled down to gain entry. Inside the house they had stolen spoons, thrown books about, stolen a watch and other valuables, and from the kitchen suits of clothes and other property of the servants was also missing. Suspicion fell on a group of rogues who had been drinking at a beer house in the village on the evening in question. A number of them were recognised and named. Davis and Evitt were taken while 'under the hands of a barber' at Thrapstone. Douse was spotted at Stukeley. He ran off across the fields, climbed over a high brick wall and swam across a river, but after running 2 miles was tired out and attempted to hide in a thicket where he was taken. Many of the goods stolen from the house and some of the clothes were found in the posession of these men; they made no defence in court and a sentence of death was recorded against them.

9 MARCH 1832

The trial of Henry Russell (32), former gaoler at Northamptonshire County Gaol, was heard at the Huntingdon Spring Assizes in a courtroom 'crowded to suffocation'. Russell was charged with being an accessory before the fact in the suicide of Mary Wormsley (23). Mary had worked as servant for Russell and his wife while he was at the gaol; it was alleged they had an affair and she fell pregnant. It was then alleged he had bought arsenic had persuaded Mary that the powder would cause a miscarriage. Russell had visited the girl on the afternoon of her death; she had gone out and returned with a white powder on her lips. Soon struck down in agony and died a short while later. Russell implored the jury 'to dismiss from their minds all the idle tales that had been circulated against him, in newspapers and in ballads.' He swore he was not responsible for her death. Russell was given character references by thirty-five witnesses showing him to be 'of the first respectability'. The jury returned a verdict of 'guilty of giving arsenic to her to produce miscarriage, but not to kill the deceased,' but still the death sentence was passed upon him. The jury petitioned the Attorney-General, while another petition against the death sentence was headed by the signatures of Mary's surviving mother, father and two sisters. Russell was saved from the gallows and his sentence commuted.

10 MARCH 1846

The Vice Chancellor of Cambridge University and the Heads of thirteen other colleges warned students not to take part in any disorderly proceedings and magistrates swore in a number of special constables to help maintain order in the town after two major disturbances on 6 March during the exhibition of the American dwarf Tom Thumb were followed by more disturbances over the following two nights. Students clashed with police at a number of locations, including Rose Crescent, Market Hill and the Petty Cury. Many windows were smashed at Christ's, Emmanuel, Pembroke and Sidney Sussex Colleges. PC John Freestone was dismissed for his conduct during these disturbances; at the Lent Assizes Freestone was found guilty of assault upon Arthur Walsh, a student of Trinity College, and was sent to prison for fourteen days.

11 MARCH 1783

George Mean was sentenced to death at the County Assizes after being convicted of the murder of George Cooper. He was not kept waiting long in the condemned cell, for only four days later he was executed upon Castle Hill, Cambridge.

12 MARCH 1811

George and Joseph Langman, who lived together with their families and servants at Downham, sent to their brother-in-law, Michael Whiting, a grocer and Methodist minister, to borrow a loaf of bread. Whiting brought them some flour and pork, from which the housekeeper made two puddings, but observed the flour would not properly adhere; she left them in a kneading trough, and the Langmans boiled one of them for dinner. The diners had hardly swallowed two or three mouthfuls before they were seized

A handbill for the exhibition of
Tom Thumb at Cambridge, 1846.

with violent vomiting. Suspecting the pudding was poisoned, one of the Langmans gave a piece to a sow in the yard, which, shortly after, was taken sick and died.

The remnants of the pudding were analysed by Mr Woolaston, a Cambridge University professor of chemistry, and were found to contain a considerable quantity of corrosive sublimate of mercury. Brought before the Ely Assizes, Whiting claimed he had laid some *nux vomica* to poison vermin and that some of it must have accidentally been carried into his flour-bin. Mr Woolaston stated that the pudding contained no other poisonous ingredient than corrosive sublimate. The prisoner, who sold drugs in his store, owned a considerable quantity of that poison. It also transpired that immediately upon its being discovered that the Langmans had been poisoned, Whiting had emptied his flour bins and washed them out. The jury found Whiting guilty and the judge passed sentence of death.

13 MARCH Punishments of the Past: The Scold's Bridle

One of the banes of Early Modern British life was the scold – nagging wife, rumourmonger or malicious village gossip. The judiciary, with its usual robust

The Scold's Bridle.

approach to such social problems, devised the Brank or Scold's Bridle. There were several different designs, but the basic construction consisted of a lockable iron framework in the form of a helmet-shaped cage that fitted tightly over the head. An aperture was provided for the mouth with a small, flat metal plate protruding into the unfortunate woman's mouth to hold her tongue down and prevent speech – hence the term 'hold your tongue!' Such devices were known to have been in use across the country until the late eighteenth century.

14 MARCH 1836

John Chapman appeared before Huntingdon Assizes for entering the farmhouse of William Rowell in a 'lonesome' part of Ramsey Fen. Chapman had, until the previous summer, been employed by Mr Rowell as a household servant, but had been dismissed after allegedly robbing his master of a pocketbook containing fourteen sovereigns, which he claimed he had found after Mr Rowell offered a reward for its discovery. Whether he was innocent of this or not, the following November an intruder was heard in the dead of night by Mrs Rowell. She had heard the stairs creak under the weight of footsteps and even heard breathing in the darkness. She made a grab towards where she thought the person was standing, but he eluded her and made his escape. However, he left behind his shoes and cap, which were recognised by the Rowells and other servants as belonging to Chapman. When traced, Chapman could not provide a satisfactory account of where he was on the night in question and was brought to trial. The evidence weighed against him, Chapman was found guilty, and a sentence of death was recorded.

15 MARCH 1836

A number of men were brought before the assizes charged with riot and assault at Woodhurst. On 11 August 1838, about forty men of Woodhurst, armed with cudgels, pitchforks and pea hooks, marched to Mr W. Fyson's Farm and demanded that the Irish labourers he was using on his farm for the harvest instead of the local men be 'sent out of the village'. Fyson refused, so the mob descended on the barn where the Irishmen were staying. The Irish fled via the back door, but James Murray was unfortunate enough to get caught. A blow was aimed at his head with a pea hook. Murray raised an arm in defence against what would have probably proved to be a fatal blow and his arm was severely cut. Another Irishman had a near escape from the thrust of a pitchfork and suffered deep penetrating wounds in each hand as he grabbed the tines to stop the thrust.

At the trial most of the men were found guilty of riot and assault and a variety of prison sentences were handed down; Joseph Elsom and John Hall were found guilty of cutting and wounding James Murray and sentenced to death.

16 MARCH 1901

Published in the *Daily News* on this day was the strange case of Lavinia Farrar (72), a blind woman 'of independent means' who had been found dead on her kitchen floor with her face bruised and nose broken. A bloodstained knife was found near the body and there were drops of blood on the floor. The body was dressed and it was not until the post-mortem that any wound was discovered. At the inquest, two doctors testified that the woman had been stabbed in the heart, but there was no puncture in any of the four garments she was wearing over the area. It would not have been possible for the woman to have stabbed herself while undressed and then put her clothes on, because the stab to the heart would have caused almost instantaneous death. A knife could not have been inserted through openings in the garments; their fastenings were too far apart. The blood on the knife and drops of blood on the floor were apparently not from the woman's wound; her wound was almost bloodless, only her innermost garment was very slightly bloodstained. There appeared to have been no robbery or motive for an attack. The jury returned an open verdict.

17 MARCH 1780

Execution of Elizabeth Butchill. At about 11 a.m. on the morning of Friday 7 January 1780, the body of a new-born female infant was found in the river near Trinity College toilets. At the inquest Mr Bond, a surgeon, deposed that he was of the opinion that the child was born alive, and received its death by the wounds in the head. Upon hearing a child had been found, William Hall suspected his niece and sent for a surgeon to examine her. In a voluntary confession, Elizabeth Butchill confessed that she had delivered herself of a female child on Thursday morning, at about half past six o'clock. The child cried some little time after its birth; and, about twenty minutes after, she had thrown the said infant down one of the holes of the necessary into the river, and buried the placenta in the dunghill near the house. Upon this evidence the coroner's jury brought a verdict of 'wilful murder' and she was committed to the Castle. Tried and found guilty, Judge Buller sentenced Elizabeth to be executed the succeeding Friday 17 March 1780, and her body to be anatomized.

18 MARCH 1841

Houghton farmer and cow leech James Inglett (94) was indicted at Huntingdon Assizes for feloniously killing Elizabeth Harlett, by administering to her a quantity of arsenic in the liquid medicines he had prepared for her. No suspicion had initially been attached to her death, but the local rumour mill ground into action and James Inglett was hounded like a witch. The coroner ordered an exhumation and a jury summoned. Two surgeons examined the disinterred body and found it in a generally healthy state, but the stomach and bowels were much inflamed. The jury returned a verdict that Elizabeth had died from 'the incautious and improper administration' by the prisoner of 'a certain noxious, inflammatory and dangerous thing, to the jurors unknown.' Further tests identified the 'dangerous thing' as arsenic. Evidence given by a chemist's shopman revealed Inglett had bought 1oz of arsenic three or four months previously. As he was in the habit of using that drug in the manufacture of his cattle ointments, the purchase excited no suspicion at the time. Lord Chief Justice Tindal told the jury that they would have to decide if Hartlett had died from the taking of arsenic, and whether the prisoner had administered it. If they were satisfied of those two facts, they would then have to say whether the prisoner had conducted himself so rashly and with such gross negligence as made him liable to an indictment for manslaughter. The jury returned a verdict of 'manslaughter'. The judge felt that, at Inglett's time of life, it would be a useless cruelty to inflict a severe punishment upon him and, considering he had been already in gaol six weeks, a sentence of fourteen days' imprisonment was passed.

19 MARCH 1819

Reports were published of the Spring Assizes at Cambridge, where John Macquire and Michael Codey were tried before Baron Graham for trying to pass forged Bank of England pound notes at Ickleton. The facts were proved; His Lordship pronounced sentence of death on them both, but 'gave Codey reason to expect that the dreadful sentence would not be carried into execution upon him, he having pleaded guilty to a minor offence.' The judge gave Macquire no hope of mercy.

20 MARCH 1836

The Honey Trap. Hugh Fletcher, Thomas Pepper, George Benford, James Heley and Emma Heley, a woman 'of infamous character', were brought before the assizes, charged with the assault and robbery of William Ratcliff on the King's highway near Cambridge. After buying drinks for Heley at the Anchor and the Chip Axe pubs, she persuaded Ratcliff to go down a dark lane with her by the side of Trinity College. Suddenly she wrested Ratcliff's stick from him, made a signal and a group of the men from the pub came running, foremost among them Hugh Fletcher, who dealt Ratcliff a formidable blow which knocked him to the ground and said, 'I'll teach you to interfere with my wife.' Then the group set about Ratcliff, kicking and beating him mercilessly. The few shillings and items he had in his pockets, his hat and cane were all taken by the gang before they disappeared into the night. A man from Trinity found Ratcliff weltering in his gore on the ground, took him back to the Anchor pub to recover where, lo and behold, some of his assailants soon walked in afterward, still streaked with blood from the fight and even carrying the stick and hat they had robbed from Ratcliff. PC Faiers was summoned and soon the miscreants were in custody. After eight weeks in hospital Ratcliff recovered and saw his assailants brought to court. The prisoners showed 'hardened and disgusting indifference' throughout the proceedings, and conducted themselves with the greatest insolence. James Heley was acquitted through lack of evidence and Thomas Pepper was acquitted on a technicality, but Hugh Fletcher, George Benford and Emma Heley were all found guilty. Justice Gaselee pronounced sentence of death on all three.

21 MARCH 1836

Mary Stoney (24) was brought before Cambridge Assizes accused of stealing an ermine muff and mantilla worth £8. Miss Stoney, 'a respectable looking woman with ladylike deportment', had gone to Stephen Thrower's drapers near King's College and selected two muffs and two mantillas. She claimed they were to be a present from her brother and she could not decide without consulting him. A man was sent round with the goods accordingly. He had been instructed not to leave the items without money, but when he arrived at her lodgings, Stoney was not there so he left them. When Stoney returned, she told her landlady she wished to 'take a stroll in Trinity'; instead she made directly for the Huntingdon Road and was picked up by the Wisbech coach. Luckily, Mr Thrower had got one of his staff to keep watch for her and she was soon in custody. Found guilty, Mary Stoney was transported for seven years.

22 MARCH 1839

Sarah Ricketts (19) was brought before Huntingdon Assizes charged with administering two drachms of arsenic to Eliza, wife of William Gale, with intent to murder her. On the conclusion of the evidence presented to the court, the judge said he thought it was impossible for the jury to convict Sarah Ricketts because she too had drunk the milk in which the poison was found, to the extent her life was also in peril, and her 'extraordinary want of care in disposing of poison in various parts of the prosecutors house, rendered a conviction in this case most unsafe, if not impossible.' No motive for murder was established either and, accordingly, Sarah Ricketts was acquitted.

23 MARCH 1844

Reports published of the Spring Assizes stated that Gifford White (18) was indicted for unlawfully sending to farmer Isaac Ilett a threatening letter on 28 December last, which read:

> Bluntisham, Hunts
> We are determined to set fire to the whole of this place if you don't set us to work, and burn you in your beds if there is not an alteration. What do you think the young men are to do if you don't set them to work. They must do something. The fact is, we cannot go any longer. We must commit robbery and everything that is contrary to your wish.
> I am,
> AN ENEMY

White was identified as the perpetrator and he confessed his guilt. The judge described the crime of sending such a letter as one of 'the greatest magnitude and enormity ... calculated to hold the district in which he lived in continual terror,' and sentenced White to be 'transported beyond the sea for the remainder of his life.'

24 MARCH 1837

Elizabeth Sellis, 'a mild-looking girl' (16), daughter of an Ely labourer, was brought before the Cambridge Assizes for the murder of her illegitimate child by cutting off its head. Towards the end of 1836 it had become noticeable that she was pregnant, but around the month of February the outward signs of the pregnancy disappeared. Shortly after this time her father gave up the occupation of the house and they moved to another part of the city. The new tenant was a Mr Veal, who decided to thoroughly empty the privy before he took possession. Almost as soon as he began his work he struck what he thought was 'a football', which proved to be the head of an infant. A further search revealed the body wrapped in part of an old gown.

At the inquest a neighbour, Mrs Jackson, testified that she had seen Miss Sellis return to the house a short while after her father had vacated it and was observed going to and from the privy on a number of occasions. Whilst the coroner's jury were inquiring into these matters, Miss Sellis made a voluntary confession, recorded in the press of the time as 'not fit for publication'. Miss Sellis drew considerable sympathy; the jury found her not guilty of murder but guilty of concealing the birth. She was sentenced to two years' imprisonment.

25 MARCH 1844

Reports published of Cambridge Assizes recount the attack on William Brown, the Isleham constable. It was the practice of the lawman to visit the public houses in the district at 11 o'clock each night in order to see that they were cleared of customers. On the night of 24 March, Brown had called at the Harp Inn and saw out the last of the drinkers. Most left quietly but a number of them loitered outside 'kicking up a row'. Constable Brown asked the men to disperse, but they refused. He ordered them to go home; they argued that they had as much right to the highway as anyone else, so the Constable threatened them with the cage. The men retorted they would not be placed there by anybody in Isleham.

The situation escalated and one of the aggressors knocked down the constable and kicked him. Constable Brown called for assistance 'in the Queen's name', but one of the men told him to go to hell and delivered him a violent blow, the rest set about the constable with punches and kicks then left him lying in the dirt. The landlord of the Harp helped the beaten constable inside and tended to his wounds. Not sated by their last attack, because they had not 'done for him', the men returned to the pub and gave the constable a few 'parting salutes', and even lingered outside to give him some more when he came outside again. Constable Brown was badly wounded, he was put to a bed and the village surgeon summoned. His injuries threatened such pressure to his brain that he was lucky to keep his life. Constable Brown recognised his assailants as Charles Whiterod, Joseph and Elijah Brown. Brought before the assizes and found guilty, these violent men were sentenced to be transported for fifteen years.

26 MARCH 1839

Cornelius, Francis and William Smith, and John and William Taylor were brought before the assizes for robbing William Smith on the King's Highway. Mr Smith, a farmer of Histon, was returning from the great horse fair at Cambridge when five gypsies came out of the darkness, held up his horse, caused Smith to become dismounted and, despite a fierce struggle, managed to pinion him and steal two sovereigns, some silver and the watch from his pocket. Stuffing Smith's mouth, the robbers then made off across the fields. The men suspected of the crime were arrested at their encampment on Arbury Meadows, but at their trial it was soon proved the night had been too dark for a full and positive identification of the accused. Although there was 'great suspicion' attached to them, in the absence of more solid evidence they were acquitted.

27 MARCH 1843

Reports were published of an extraordinary case brought before the assizes of John Frederick Mortlock, who was indicted for shooting at and wounding his uncle, Edmond Mortlock, a resident fellow of Christ's College. John Mortlock's father had died some years previously and young John had developed a grievance against his uncle over what he considered was 'his' property and money. The uncle seemed to have helped the boy out with money as and when he asked for it, but his behaviour, demands and accusations had become more and more aggressive. John had taken rooms at the Eagle, but after a week a wrangle occurred after which John was asked to leave by the landlord, Mr Mitchell. Mitchell then went to see John's uncle Edmond at his rooms at Christ's College. Shortly after his arrival, John Mortlock burst in and advanced to his uncle, pointing a pistol at him. John pulled the trigger, the cap exploded, but miraculously the pistol did not go off. John then drew a dagger; Mr Mitchell picked up a poker, but was put to flight as John threatened him too. Revd Mortlock picked up his chair to defend himself. John sprang up, caught him by the collar, and pointed the pistol at the Revd, saying, 'You've robbed me of my property.' Revd Mortlock said he did not have any of his property, but John snarled, 'I am determined to shoot you, and to blow out your brains!' Mr Cartmell, a tutor at the college, entered the room. On seeing him, John Mortlock lowered his pistol and it went off close to the Revd's body, to which the cleric cried, 'O God! You've killed me.' Mortlock released his uncle and went to an adjoining room.

Cartmell got Mortlock to his rooms and they found he had only suffered a flesh wound. John Mortlock then joined two hunting whips together, lowered himself down from the window to the courtyard below, and made his escape along the river.

In his flight Mortlock, came across Thomas Leech, who was checking his eel traps. Mortlock fired his pistol at Leach, who 'felt something hit him,' but he suffered no wound. Leach apprehended Mortlock and took him to the authorities. At his trial, John Mortlock addressed the jury at length about his grievances; some may have felt sympathy for his frustration but they still found him guilty of grievous bodily harm and sentenced him to transportation for fifteen years.

28 MARCH 1812

William Nightingale, alias Bird (29), was executed for forging and uttering a £5 note purporting to be from the Windsor and Berkshire Bank. At his trial it had been ascertained that Nightingale had gone to the Black Lion pub in Cambridge with his brother the previous February and both had enjoyed a fine dinner, for which he paid with the note in question. When tendered at the bank, the note was declared a forgery.

During their meal the brothers had been heard to mention Godmanchester, and the constables were despatched on fast horses and arrested the brothers there. Taken back to Cambridge, both were put on trial, but it was soon clear that William was the real culprit and his brother walked free. The printing plates from which the note was forged were presented in court and it was soon revealed that William had lived for a good six months off the proceeds of forged notes. Found guilty in the face of overwhelming evidence, Nightingale was executed on 28 March 1812 upon the Cambridge gallows, 'in the presence of an immense concourse of spectators, who were deeply affected at the awful and melancholy scene.'

29 MARCH 1844

Reports circulate of a fatal accident that befell Mr Edward Jones Fox of St John's College. While driving a phaeton-and-pair along the Trumpington Road, Fox, with three of his friends, was approaching the stone bridge when the horses began to pull. Instead of pulling them up gradually, he put his leg across the reins; the reigns broke and the horses made off at full speed. Fox leapt from his seat, appearing to land on his feet after a glancing a blow to his head. He walked a few paces, but then said he could go no more and was assisted onto the wayside. Mr Bailey Turner, a surgeon, was passing in his gig. He stopped and was in the process of taking Fox to the Cambridge Hospital when the

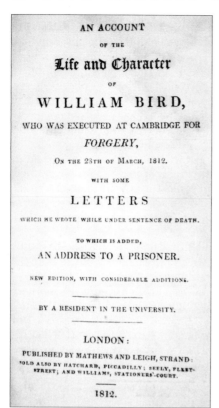

AN ACCOUNT

OF THE

Life and Character

OF

WILLIAM BIRD,

WHO WAS EXECUTED AT CAMBRIDGE FOR

FORGERY,

ON THE 23TH OF MARCH, 1812.

WITH SOME

LETTERS

WHICH HE WROTE WHILE UNDER SENTENCE OF DEATH.

TO WHICH IS ADDED,

AN ADDRESS TO A PRISONER.

NEW EDITION, WITH CONSIDERABLE ADDITIONS.

BY A RESIDENT IN THE UNIVERSITY.

LONDON:

PUBLISHED BY MATHEWS AND LEIGH, STRAND;
SOLD ALSO BY HATCHARD, PICCADILLY; SEELY, FLEET-
STREET; AND WILLIAMS, STATIONERS'-COURT.

1812.

The published account of The Life and Character of William Bird, *1812.*

latter was suddenly seized by violent convulsions and threw himself over the wheel. Taken to a nearby house, he died the same night. A post-mortem examination showed that he died from 'concussion of the brain.'

30 MARCH 1833

Poachers William Westnott and Charles Carter were executed at Cambridge Castle Gaol for the murder of William Kidd, assistant keeper for the Earl of Hardwicke in Kingston Wood, Wimpole on 5 January. Kidd had been shot, but lived long enough to identify his attackers. William Westnott (24), Charles Carter (22), and Charles Allgood (42) were brought up at the assizes. Westnott and Carter were found guilty of the shooting, but Allgood was reprieved from the death sentence as His Lordship wished to make some discrimination in the case; Allgood was in the wood 'for an improper purpose', but had not drawn a trigger against Kidd. Westnott and Carter were hanged before a large crowd, who were noted for their 'respectful quiet', with the exception of the shrieks of Carter's sister. Carter appeared to die instantly, whereas Westnott struggled violently for several minutes before the noose strangled him.

31 MARCH 1792

Jeremiah Archer was executed on this date upon Castle Hill, Cambridge after being tried and found guilty of arson at the County Assizes.

APRIL

*Matthew Hopkins, Witchfinder General. In April 1646 Hopkins was summoned to Huntingdonshire
'to search for evil disposed persons called witches.' Capitalizing on local Puritan fears and prejudices, the
women he searched were often old, marginal members of society upon whom some locals bore a grudge
or wanted to find a scapegoat for the untimely loss of a relative or livestock, personal illness, injury or
misfortune. Employed by the worthy citizens of towns and villages across East Anglia, Hopkins sent more
witches to the gallows than any other witch hunter in England and made himself a fortune in the process.
Extant and verified records state he was responsible for seventy-four executions for witchcraft and thirty-
six deaths in gaol, but the actual figure was probably considerably higher. Folklore likes to tell of Hopkins
being suspected of being a witch himself and punished accordingly, but the truth is he died of consumption.*

1 APRIL 1756

A village in Cambridge or a town of impudence? A curious print entitled 'THE PUZZLE' was published in 1756 showing a tall headstone inscription being poured over by learned gentlemen. The script under the title states, 'To the penetrating geniuses of Oxford, Cambridge, Eton, Westminster and the learned Society of Antiquarians. This curious inscription is humbly dedicated. Printed for J. Bowles at No. 43 in Cornhill and Carrington Bowles No. 69 in St Paul Churchyard London.' The first, fourth, sixth and three concluding lines are imitations of a Latin inscription, but it is, in fact, a simple English epitaph, the key published shortly afterwards tells the reader to ignore the stops, capital letters or division of the words – the inscription then reads:

> Beneath this stone reposeth Claud Coster, Tripe-seller of Impington as does his consort Jane.

Whether this did indeed refer to the Cambridge village or infers a place of origin fraught with mischief, impudence or trickery, has never been revealed, neither has the man – or woman – who created THE PUZZLE.

The mysterious eighteenth-century print entitled 'The Puzzle'.

2 APRIL

In the days when the county assize could mean death to those found guilty, 2 and 3 April proved to be 'Hanging Days'. On this day in 1763, for example, William Johnson was executed upon Castle Hill, Cambridge for housebreaking. In 1785, upon this same day, a massive crowd watched a double execution as Thomas Ashe was hanged for highway robbery and John Hopper struggled against the ever tightening rope for burglary.

3 APRIL, 1779

Thomas Dellar was hanged upon Castle Hill, Cambridge for stealing sheep. On this same day and location in 1802 William Wright and John Bullock were hanged for creating forged Bank of England notes. In 1824 John Lane (25) swung for rape at Cheveley. At the last moment upon the gallows he declared himself innocent; the trap door still fell.

In 1830 William Reader (26) and William Turner (22) were executed, having been found guilty of setting fire to a stack of haulm and a barn, the property of Mr William Chalk of Linton. The reason for the attack was the reaction of these two men to words overheard through the vestry window of the Meeting House, where Chalk said he was not afraid of any man and they thought he should be and fired his stack. David Howard (23) had also been found guilty of firing stacks at Badlingham and he too joined Read and Turner on the castle gallows on this day. Brought out on to the scaffold, the three men embraced and then gave a final bow to the multitude watching. The ropes were then adjusted, the executioner gave the signal, the trap fell and the three men 'appeared to die instantly and almost without a struggle'. After hanging the usual time the bodies were taken away by friends and family for interment in their respective parishes.

4 APRIL, 1850

The Great Fire of Cottenham. The alarm was raised after two adjoining barns belonging to Mr Freeman Goode and Mr Thomas Graves were found on fire. A strong breeze fanned the flames from the west and the fire spread at a terrifying pace. Local labourers and gownsmen from Cambridge attempted to quell the fire, but their efforts 'were so manifestly unavailing, that people at last stood by in helpless and despairing inaction.' Fortunately no human lives were lost, but many houses, pubs, barns and buildings were destroyed and a vast quantity of livestock killed. The suspected arsonist was William Hayward, who had been lodging at the Lamb Inn whilst doing casual labour for farmer Thomas Graves. The landlord claimed Hayward had said to him, 'I have been a match for old Graves ... damn and blast the fire: I wish it would burn half Cottenham down.'

The morning after the fire, the landlord woke to discover Hayward had fled. Hayward was tracked down and faced a trial at the forthcoming assizes, but, for want of firm evidence or witnesses, who actually saw Hayward start the fire, the bill was ignored by the Grand Jury.

5 APRIL, 1913

The Cambridge Murders. Hungarian-born Captain Albert Paul Schule (56) grew up in Germany, enlisted in the Prussian Army and served through the Franco Prussian war. After struggling in business in London he moved his family to Cambridge, where he eked out a living as a private German tutor and became 'an advanced spiritualist'.

Mrs Schule and her baby had died during childbirth the previous February. In an attempt to save her life the doctor present had given Mrs Schule chloroform. Captain Schule believed the chloroform would kill her because he had 'seen it in the crystal and also in the horoscope' and claimed it would 'destroy her astral body and brain.' The nurse noticed Schule giving his wife a capsule that he said contained an antidote (but she did not report this to the doctor). Mrs Schule died twenty minutes later.

The whole affair clearly weighed heavily on Schule's mind until he became so unstable he wrote two letters, one to a friend; another to the Chief Constable. Schule wrote, 'Grief, indignation and despair at the unnatural, horrible death of my wife has already broken down my already intensely suffering constitution and at last overthrown my mind. I cannot stand this terrible strain any longer, so I depart this life, taking with me my dear children ...'. He concluded, 'I forbid every medical man to interfere with my or my children's body [sic] and I trust the last will of a broken man will be respected.' Schule shot his children and himself with a revolver at their Regent Street home. At the inquest the jury returned a verdict of 'murders and suicide during temporary insanity.'

6 APRIL, 1593

Witches of Warboys hanged for witchcraft. This tragic story began when Jane Throckmorton (9) suffered a prolonged sneezing session, went into a trance, and suffered convulsions when she heard church bells. Her concerned parents sent to Cambridge for Dr Barrow who, after three consultations, found nothing untoward and suggested they obtain a second opinion. Dr Butler of Clare College was called, who 'verily thought there was some kind of witchcraft wrought towards this child.' Jane thought her neighbour, Mrs Alice Samuel (60), looked like a witch and soon believed it must have been Mrs Samuel who had cursed her.

Soon the other Throckmorton girls developed similar 'convulsions'. Sir Henry and Lady Cromwell (Oliver Cromwell's grandmother) of Ramsey visited the Throckmortons. Lady Cromwell confronted Mrs Samuel, who denied the allegations of witchcraft, saying, 'Lady, why do you use me thus, I never did you any harm as yet.' That night Lady

A witch feeding her imps.

Cromwell had a nightmare during which a cat belonging to Mother Samuel 'offered to pluck off all the skin and flesh from her body.' Her health went into decline and she died fifteen months later.

In October 1592 the Throckmorton girls' convulsions became worse. They told their father their condition would not improve unless he employed Alice Samuel as a servant. Their wish was granted and the torment and allegations of witchcraft against Alice began again and included such accusations as; she was suckling her imps through a cut on her chin, and she only left the hall to feed the 'evil sprits' she kept in a chest.

On 26 December 1592 Robert Throckmorton came to the Samuel's house with two constables to escort Alice and her daughter, Agnes, to Buckden, where the Bishop of Lincoln conducted an inquisition. Three days later the Bishop was joined by JPs Francis Cromwell and Richard Tryce. Under pressure, Alice confessed a diabolical pact and told how a strange man had sent 'devils' to her in the form of chickens which she named Pluck, Catch, White and Smack. Alice and Agnes were remanded to Huntingdon Gaol. Agnes had been implicated by association so she was bailed on condition she stayed at the Throckmortons. Allegations of witchcraft were soon made against her. Joan Throckmorton claimed the nosebleeds she suffered were evidence of the evil spirits Agnes had sent to her. Mary Throckmorton scratched Agnes's face, it did not bleed; instead 'water' came out of it and this 'proved' Agnes was a witch.

After this incident John Samuel went to the manor, where Mrs Throckmorton accused him of being a witch and he was forced to pronounce himself so. On 4 April 1593 all three Samuels were brought before the Huntingdon Assizes. When asked for his plea, John Samuel declared 'not guilty.' Justice Fenner took offence and warned John if he continued to deny the charges he would find him guilty and sentence him to death at that moment, John pled 'guilty' and the rest of the family followed his lead. Convicted of bewitching Lady Cromwell to death and causing the affliction of the Throckmorton children, John, Alice and Agnes Samuel were hanged at Huntingdon. Their property was confiscated and sold, to pay for a sermon against witchcraft to be preached every year in All Saint's Church, Huntingdon. This practice continued for just over 200 years, until accusations of witchcraft against Ann Izzard at Great Paxton in 1808 ended up in legal action and gaol for some of her accusers; only then were the sermons abandoned.

7 APRIL 1787

Solomon Tuck executed at Ely for the murder of John Saunders (40). The Saunders family lived at the inn on St German's Bridge near Wisbech. One night, local rake and one-time landlord at Downham Bridge Tuck walked into the pub and asked for a bed for the night. Whether it was passion at first glance or a contrived meeting is unclear, but that same night John Saunders' wife, Mary, snuck into Tuck's bed. Tuck became so enamoured by Mary all he could think of after was how he could be rid of John Saunders. He tried to pay a local man and even another guest to do the dirty work for him, but they both declined.

On 25 February 1787, Tuck and John Saunders left St German's Bridge for the Crown and Mitre at Leverington, where Tuck plied Saunders with alcohol until he was drunk. Tuck returned to St German's later that night, clearly intoxicated and claiming Saunders had disappeared after being indecisive of where he wanted to go next. He was concerned Saunders may have drowned.

A month later, a bargeman found the bloated, decomposing body of Saunders near the Horse Shoe Hole, Wisbech. A number of pre-mortem wounds and bruises were noted when the body was examined. Tuck was arrested and brought before the Spring Assizes, where the two men he had tried to co-opt for the murder came forward and testified. Found guilty of murder, Tuck was hanged before a large crowd and his body later conveyed to surgeons for dissection.

Three on the gallows – all of them hanged for witchcraft.

8 APRIL, Cambridgeshire Death and Burial Rites

Unclaimed bodies from rivers, executed felons and suicides were all fair game for the dissectionists' table, but such legitimate supplies by no means met the demands of the medical schools, thus a dark business soon emerged – bodysnatching. In April 1732 a grave was found robbed in Ditton churchyard and it was rumoured the body had been delivered to Emmanuel College. Obtaining a warrant, a large number of Ditton folk marched on the college, but were refused entry. The mob then attacked the walls. The students rose up to defend their territory and violence erupted. The situation was so severe that the Town Clerk read the Riot Act, only then would the mob disperse. Later, Justice of the Peace Mr Pern granted a warrant for constables to search the entire college. No body was discovered, but the following morning the unfortunate corpse was found floating in the pond of the college close.

Bodysnatchers about their dark business.

9 APRIL, 1646

Witch Hunt in Huntingdonshire. Frances Moore was brought before Nicholas Pedley, one of His Majesty's Justices of Peace for Huntingdonshire, to give testimony upon her involvement in witchcraft. In her statements she claimed to have been given a black puppy by Margaret Simson of Great Catworth, which she had named 'Pretty'. Simson told her if she cursed any cattle and set the same dog upon them, they 'would presently die.' Goodwife Weed gave Moore a white cat, telling her that if she would deny God, and affirm the same by her blood, then whomsoever she cursed and sent that cat unto, they would die shortly after. Moore then confessed that she did deny God, and in affirmation of this she pricked her finger with a thorn, it issued blood, which the cat presently licked. Goodwife Weed had named the cat Tissy.

Moore claimed that after an altercation with William Foster she sent the white cat to him, he immediately fell sick and, after writhing in agony for days, died. Moore also stated that on a separate occasion, when cows belonging to Edward Hulls and Peter Browne

Witches on their broomsticks. A devil is also close at hand.

had wandered and eaten her grain, she set Pretty on them and the poor beasts 'swelled and died shortly after.' Moore concluded her statement claiming she had killed her dog and cat about a year previously, but added after that the same dog and cat 'haunted her familiarly' and when she was apprehended 'they crept under her clothes, and tortured her so that she could not speak to confess freely.'

10 APRIL, Grim Tales of Cambridgeshire: The Bailiff of Marshland

Asthma and ague were common maladies in the Fens. In his *History of Imbanking and Drayning* (1662) William Dugdale described the Fen folk's environment: 'There is no element good, the air being for the most part cloudy, gross and full of rotten harrs; the water putrid and muddy, yea, full of loathsome vermin; the earth spungy and boggy.' In *The Cambridge, Ely and King's Lynn Road* (1902) Charles Harper explained:

> No wonder, then, that the terrible disease of ague seized upon the unfortunate inhabitants of this watery waster. Few called this miasmic condition by name, preferring to call it the Bailiff of Marshland. To be arrested by this dread bailiff was a frequent experience for those who worked early or late in the marshes, when the poisonous vapours still lingered. To alleviate the miseries of ague the Fen-folk resorted to opium, and often became slaves to that drug.

11 APRIL, 1829

Execution of William Osborne for highway robbery. David Darwood, a higgler from Warboys, stopped at the Three Horse Shoes at Knapwell. He left well fed and refreshed and was travelling along the road to Conington when a man he recognised from his dress as having left the pub shortly before him, came out from the gloom with the demand 'Stand and deliver your money!' Darwood insisted he had no money. The highwayman replied, 'I know you have and I will have it,' and then struck Darwood about the head with a heavy weapon – probably the dibbing iron Darwood had seen in the hand of the man in the pub.

Darwood was beaten and dragged to a dike where he was thrown over and his breeches pocket rifled and robbed of 12 sovereigns, a bank note and a letter. Darwood was then delivered a great blow across the head and left for dead in the as and the robber made off. Darwood had got a good look at the man's features in the moonlight and previously at the pub. Darwood saw him two days later at Conington and thus William Osborne was taken into custody and later tried and found guilty. In the condemned cell, Osborne acknowledged he committed the offence and expressed his regret of the crime. Osborne ate a large breakfast on his last morning and was executed in front of Cambridge Castle Gaol. After hanging for the usual hour, his body was taken to his native village of Boxworth.

12 APRIL, Grim Tales of Cambridgeshire: Fen Women

In 1774, Lord Orford set out with a fleet of nine ships to explore the Fens with the same sense of adventure one may have recorded for a voyage and exploration of Darkest Africa. On Whittlesea Mere a storm blew up and a number of the adventurers were seasick. In the account of the voyage it was recorded of Outwell: 'It is equally remarkable for the ugliness of the inhabitants as for the handsomeness of the church – a disagreeable sallow complexion, broad flat nose and wide mouth predominating among them.' Lord Orford noted 'Many very old women in Upwell, Outwell and March; the sex in general extremely ugly.'

13 APRIL, 1850

The last public double execution at Cambridge Castle. Castle Camps farm labourer Elias Lucas (25) and his sister-in-law Mary Reeder (20) were hanged for the murder of Elias's wife, Susan, by the administration of two drams of arsenic. It was the old story of an illicit affair but their desire to remove the obstacle to their union, was this time made more perverse because the unwanted wife and mistress were sisters. Mary was poisoned at a meal she had shared with Elias and Mary. Complaining the food tasted bitter, she was soon vomiting and forced to take to her bed, where she died. Dr Frederick Cramer was called, but Susan was already dead when he arrived.

The symptoms shown by the body suggested cholera or poisoning; Cramer suspected the latter. Tests were carried out and arsenic was detected in her body. Elias and Mary were arrested and tried before Mr Justice Whiteman at Cambridgeshire Assizes. Both were found guilty and sentenced to death.

The hour of the execution was set for 12 noon. About 40,000 attended; stands were erected for those wanting good view, and a local landlord put up scaffolding with a commanding view of the drop and let these prime seats at 5s each. The best views were from the top of Castle Hill. Parties who had secured these places were busily engaged

George Walpole, 3rd Earl of Orford, Lord of the Bedchamber to George II and Fenland Exibition leader.

in pelting missiles upon the heads of the parties below as the pair were bought out and hanged by William Calcraft in front of the debtor's door of the Gaol on Castle Hill. After the statutory hour, the bodies were taken down, placed in coffin shells and conveyed to the women's ward and laid out. Shortly after 5 p.m. they were interred in the prison garden in the presence of some of the relatives of the deceased.

14 APRIL, Grim Tales of Cambridgeshire: Highwaymen

The Wheatsheaf in St Ives was a common resort of highwaymen in Cambridgeshire. This pub was well situated for their nefarious purposes, located as it was at the top of Alconbury Hill; the horses pulling the coaches up the Great North Road from the south would be in no fit state to be whipped up to a gallop to escape from the high ground where the highwaymen would lay in wait. One of the ostlers from the pub was said to have had a lucrative sideline in highway robbery. He would take a horse from the stable, disguise himself and use a candlestick instead of a pistol, in the gloom it would have looked like the barrel of a gun – he just had to hope no coachman or gentry inside called his bluff!

THE DYING WORDS and CONFESSION OF

Elias Lucas AND Mary Reader,

Who were Executed this morning (April 13) in front of the County Goal at Cambridge, for the wilful MURDER of SUSAN LUCAS.

LIFE, CHARACTER, &c.

TRIAL and CONVICTION.

CONFESSION

EXECUTION.

COPY OF VERSES
Written the night previous to Execution.

The broadside printed for the execution of Elias Lucas and Mary Reeder, 1850.

61

15 APRIL, 1881

To fetch a pail of water. On this day was reported the case of a fatal accident that occurred on the Ely and Newmarket railway near Soham railway station. Mr John Woodruff (80) had left his home with yoke and pails to fetch some water and was crossing the line about 150yds from the station when the passenger train from Ely, due at Soham at 5 p.m., came round the curve. Although the engine driver turned on his whistle, the old man was very deaf and kept on his way. He was caught by the engine and killed instantly. At the inquest at the Anchor Inn, before J.N. York Esq., the evidence of Mr Farmer, the engine driver, showed that he had used every effort to attract the man's attention, but in vain. The inhabitants of the neighbourhood had to cross the line by Spencers Drove to get to the river for water. After returning a verdict of 'accidentally killed', the jury strongly recommended that efforts should be made for a supply of water without crossing the rails.

16 APRIL, 1646

Witch Hunt in Huntingdonshire. During her examination before a Justice of the Peace, Jane Wallis of Keiston said as she was making her bed in her chamber when there appeared the shape of a man in black clothes, who bid her good-morrow:

A witch, a devil in the guise of a black priest and a familliar.

She asked what his name was, and he said his name was Blackeman, and asked her if she were poor, and she told him that she was; then he told her he would send one Grissell and Greedigut to her, that shall do anything for her. She said he would have lain with her, but she would not suffer him. After Blackeman was departed from her, within three or four days, Grissell and Greedigut came to her, in the shapes of dogs with great bristles of hogs' hair upon their backs, and said to her they were come from Blackeman to do what she would command them she said she lacked nothing: then they prayed her to give them some victuals, she said she was poor and had none to give them, and so they departed. 'Yet she confessed that Blackeman, Grissell, and Greedigut divers times came to her afterwards, and brought her two or three shillings at a time, and more says not.

17 APRIL, 1872

Disquiet lingered among the farm labourers of the Fen district. At Long Sutton most of the men had been out on strike. The customary hours had been from 7 to 5 from Michaelmas to Lady Day and half past 6 to 5.30 from Lady Day to Michaelmas. When 6 April passed the men who persisted in keeping the winter hours were discharged. At Sutton Bridge a number of women paraded the village with flags and banners and went to one farm and threatened the women who did not leave work. The Unionists were willing to let the farmers have the hours provided they paid extra, say a penny a mile a day, for those men with a long distance to walk.

18 APRIL,

Witch Hunt in Huntingdonshire. In the Spring of 1646 Matthew Hopkins 'The Witchfinder General' and his assistant, John Stearne, were summoned to Huntingdon after a number of confessions to the practice of witchcraft were obtained from about twenty people from the outlying villages of Great Catworth, Molesworth, Keiston and Bythorn. It is known a number of them were convicted and some, in all probability, went to the gallows, but sadly the records that could confirm this are incomplete. What is known is that Hopkins was not universally welcome as the county's saviour from witchcraft. Before he arrived, John Gaule, of Great Staughton, condemned the methods of witch finders and denounced such men as charlatans. Hopkins was thrown by this dissent and even wrote to one of Gaule's parishioners:

> I have this day received a letter to come to a Towne called Great Staughton to search for evil disposed persons called Witches (though I hear your Minister if farre against us through ignorance) I intend to come (God willing) the sooner to heare his singular Judgement on the behalf of such parties; I have known a Minister in Suffolke preach as much against their discovery in a pulpit and forc'd to recant it in the same place ...

Perhaps Hopkins was alluding to the fact that just the previous year (1645) he had extracted a confession from 80-year-old John Lowes, Rector of Brandeston, which had led to the old man's conviction and execution at the Bury St Edmunds witch trial. Gaule was not intimidated, and in *Select Cases of Conscience touching Witches and Witchcrafts* (1646), Gaule expounded his criticism of Hopkins, Stearn and other witch finders for their greed, ignorance and methods, declaring them worse symbols of rebellion and chaos than the witches upon which they made war, and expounding his conviction and abhorrence that:

The frontispiece illustration from The Discovery of Witches: In Answer to Several Queries Lately Delivered to the Judge of the Assize for the County of Norfolk *by Matthew Hopkins, 1647.*

Every old woman with a wrinkled face, a furrowed brow, a hairy lip, a gobber tooth, a squint eye, a squeaking voice or scolding tongue, having a rugged coat on her back, a skull-cap on her head, a spindle in her hand and a dog or cat by her side, is not only suspect but pronounced for a witch.

Gaule's voice of reason was not alone and underpinned a complaint that forced Hopkins to answer some challenging questions posed by the judges at Norwich. Hopkins protested his motives were both godly and sincere and claimed he had been the victim of malicious rumours. His defence was published in *The Discovery of Witches: In Answer to severall Queries Lately Delivered to the Judges of Assize for the County of Norfolk* (1647). He died the same year.

19 APRIL, 1779

James Hackman executed at Tyburn. Hackman's parents had bought him an ensign's commission in the 68th Foot. He had not been long in the Army when he was sent to command a recruiting party. While at Huntingdon he was frequently invited to dine with Lord Sandwich at Hinchingbrooke House; it was there he first became acquainted with Miss Martha Reay, an actress who was charming and beautiful and also the earl's mistress and mother of a number of his children. Hackman became obsessed with the woman and, believing she craved stability, even left the Army, took up holy orders and obtained a living with a parsonage at Wiveton in Norfolk. He wrote to Martha with the good news: 'Now my happiness can be deferred no longer. Oh, consent to marry me directly!' Martha's singing coach, Singnora Galli, informed Hackman that Martha had tired of him and had taken up with another. This was too much for Hackman. He stalked Martha to Covent Garden where, after she came out from the theatre, he pushed through the crowd and shot her in the head. He then put his other pistol to his temple, but it failed to fire. Hackman then attempted to club himself to death with the butt. Despite attracting considerable sympathy, Hackman was determined to end his life on the gallows; found guilty of murder he got his wish.

20 APRIL, 1737

Having made a nuisance of himself among the inhabitants of Cambridge wielding a sword and other offensive weapons, 'Mad Tom' (Thomas Miller) had an order made against him by the town sessions, stating, 'after this order or soon as he can be apprehended within the town, suffer the correction of whipping by the hands of the common cryer of this town, under which he is to continue until he leaves the same town.' Tom had already been in the workhouse and after being publicly whipped at the Market Cross he had been forcibly ejected from the town by the common officer. But he returned almost immediately and caused more trouble. On 11 July 1739, the justices could tolerate no more and ordered he be captured and thrown in the House of Correction 'till further order.'

21 APRIL, 1600

The First Great Fire of Gamblingay. The fire began at Avenel's Manor and rapidly spread from the north-east of the village. In a letter from the Privy Council to Sir Thomas Egerton, it was related:

*James Hackman – officer,
cleric and lovelorn murderer.*

Whereas divers of the Justices of the Peace in the countie of Cambridge have certyfied us the lamentable accydent that hath fallen upon the inhabitantes of Gamlingay ... the moste parte of the said towne to the number of 76 houses with divers barnes and stackes of corne were suddainlie consumed.

A second 'Great Fire' in 1812 was caused by sparks from the forge in Thomas Wright's wheelwright's yard, which unfortunately set light to a nearby thatched roof. The fire spread down Mill Street and destroyed twenty-two dwellings, six barns and several outbuildings. It was eventually extinguished by the horse-drawn fire engine from Potton.

22 APRIL, 1786

Simon Norris was hanged on the Ely gallows after being found guilty of stealing a sheep.

23 APRIL, 1835

Escaped convict. John Gunton, a bargeman, was being held at Huntingdon Prison under sentence for assault. Escaping at about 11 o'clock on 22 April, he was pursued by the turnkey and others over the enclosures between the prison and the town, then on to the bank of the river and towards St Ives. With his pursuers closing upon him, Dunton dived into the river and swam across. He was last seen in the Fens near Ramsey – a reward was offered for his apprehension.

24 APRIL, 1834

Robert Brigstock executed at Ely for firing a stack at March. The case was a tragic one of a young, hot-headed man who, after an argument over the standard of his ploughing on Mr Vawser's farm, in March lost his pay and his job and bore a grudge against farmer Vawser.

Months later he went drinking with former work colleague Thomas Story and a few others, ending up the worse for drink in Edgley's beer shop at Town End. In the early hours of the morning, Story and Brigstock left their pals and wandered off towards Vawser's Farm intent on revenge vandalism. Brigstock wanted to burn the hay stacks and got some coals from the hearth in his father's house. Story tried to stop him, but the coals ended up under the stack, Story tried to put them out with his cap but couldn't. He fled, but before he got home he saw the fire blazing in the distance.

PC Elliot easily tracked his first suspect; he followed the footprints he had left in the soft earth to the door of Thomas Story. Story's married sister, Sarah Hartley, had seen his charred cap and was convinced he had been responsible for the fire. Brigstock was also a name given by a few witnesses and he soon joined Story in separate cells in the village lock-up. Neither was going to tell, but Story's conscience (or fear of the noose) led him to eventually confess his part in the arson. Both men were brought before the Spring Assizes, both were found guilty but with a recommendation for mercy on account of the men both being just 19 years old. Sarah Hartley had given evidence, and believed that it was because of her statements that her brother had been sent to the gallows and she had to be assisted from the court. She died a short while later, and the day after her death the news arrived that her brother had been reprieved, but Robert Brigstock went to the gallows.

25 APRIL, 1599

Oliver Cromwell was born at Huntingdon. Educated at the Huntingdon Grammar School, Cromwell studied briefly at Sidney Sussex College, Cambridge, then married and settled in Huntingdon. He later lived in St Ives and Ely. Closely associated with Cambridgeshire throughout his life, the story of the puritan who was to lead the Parliamentary forces through the English Civil War, oversaw the beheading of Charles I and became our county's Lord Protector is well known, but few realise what happened to him after his death.

After laying in state at Somerset House, Cromwell was finally buried in Westminster Abbey near his old compatriots Henry Ireton and John Bradshaw. After the restoration, Charles II wreaked revenge on those who committed treason against his father. On 26 January 1661 the bodies of Cromwell, Ireton and Bradshaw were unceremoniously disinterred and on 30 January, the twelfth anniversary of his fathers' execution, they were drawn on a sledge to Tyburn, hanged until sun down, and then beheaded. The heads of the 'regicides', parboiled and covered in pitch, were impaled on spikes at Westminster Hall on the anniversary of Charles I's funeral. Cromwell's head remained there for over twenty

Oliver Cromwell – Lord Protector and 'Lord of the Fens'.

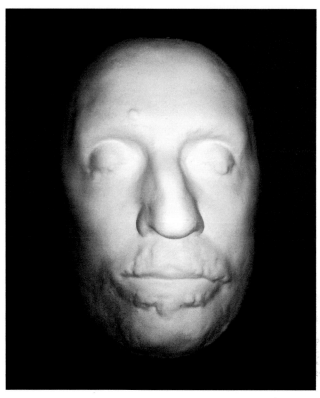

The death mask of Oliver Cromwell, warts and all.

years, until it was brought down in a gale and was picked up by a sentry. After passing through a number of hands and being exhibited in various curiosity shows, the head was given by the niece of the last show proprietor to her family doctor, Dr Josiah Henry Wilkinson, for safekeeping; she eventually sold it to him. Passing down the family line to Canon Horace Wilkinson of Woodbridge, during the 1930s, the head, still on its iron spike and fragment of wooden pole, was scientifically examined and revealed evidence of the eight axe blows used to remove Cromwell's head, his 'reddish hair' and even 'the historical wart which Cromwell insisted on his portrait painters putting in.' The nose had been flattened during the beheading, almost all the teeth were gone and the lips broken to fragments, but all the tests proved conclusively that this was indeed the head of Oliver Cromwell. Canon Wilkinson believed Cromwell's head should be given a fitting final resting place, and he presented it to Cromwell's old edifice of learning, Sidney Sussex College, Cambridge. The head resides there to this day, in a secret location known only to a few staff.

26 APRIL, 1868

Four militia recruits from Gamblingay and one from Littleport were inprisoned for seventy-two hours after being found guilty of disobeying orders by visiting Littleport, a town forbidden to them by express orders because smallpox was 'raging at that place.'

27 APRIL, 1921

Newspapers revel in the dismissal of the final appeal of the Venerable John Wakeford, Canon and Preceptor of Lincoln Cathedral. This had been his final chance to clear his name by overturning the judgement of the Consistory Court who had found him guilty, under the Clergy Discipline Act, of adultery 'with an unknown woman' at the Bull Hotel, Peterborough on Sunday 14 and Monday 15 March and Good Friday, 2 April 1920.

Archdeacon Wakeford attempted to conduct a discreet affair many miles from his diocese in Peterborough, but unfortunately for him the police were on the look-out for a fraudster who dressed as a clergyman which enabled him to easily pass dud cheques; the wanted man was also known to be accompanied by a woman. So when a clergyman in gaiters, accompanied by a woman, was seen by beat officers entering the Bull Hotel, their suspicions were aroused. Detective Sergeant King related, 'the Bull is a respectable hotel, but not the class of hotel a clergyman would use.' The hotel register was examined and, after police enquiries with the Lincoln Cathedral authorities to ascertain the identity of the 'suspicious clergyman', it became clear he was not the fraudster, but this led to questions being raised over what the Venerable John Wakeford was doing there sharing a room with a woman who was not his wife.

28 APRIL, Cures of Fenland Cunning Folk: Coughs and Colds

The most widely accepted treatment for a severe cold, and even whooping cough, were cooked mice – fried, boiled, but mostly baked. Folklorist James Wentworth Day remembered, as a lad, being fed 'a sizzling golden brown oven-baked mouse' by Old Nanny Howlett, the wise woman of Wicken Lode, when he was in bed suffering from whooping cough. Some children were fed a mouse on a regular basis in the belief it warded away sickness.

Another 'cure' for whooping cough involved the plucking of a hair from the top of the neck at the back of a sufferer's head. This would then be tied to a dog's collar, transferring the sickness to the unfortunate animal.

The mouse – fried, boiled or baked – was a Fenland cure for coughs and colds.

Perhaps the sufferer would prefer a more equine cure – inhale the breath of a stallion or if all else fails pass the patient down the body of an old horse (just in case the transferred sickness killed the animal, you were not supposed to use a good one).

29 APRIL, 1786

William Russell was hanged for highway robbery in front of a large crowd upon the Ely gallows.

30 APRIL, 1844

Thomas Parrott, a brewer's drayman of Peterborough, was crossing a bridge when he was accosted by James Wright (25), one of the 'idlers who are in the habit of hanging about the market place', who begged money to get some drink. Parrott pointed out that if Wright worked as hard as he did then he too would have some money, but he had a family to support too and walked on. Parrott crossed the Market Place and cathedral and on into the suburbs. Wright caught up with him and 'bothered' him again. Parrott firmly said no. This was met by a sharp blow from Wright that floored Mr Parrott. Wright then went through his pockets and made off with the drayman's purse. Parrott informed the police and a 'hue and cry' was raised. Wright was capture many miles from Peterborough the following day. On his way to the City Gaol he shouted to a friend, 'tell my mother not to buy a counsellor,' as he wanted to be found guilty and join a couple of his mates who had been sent to Botany Bay! He got his wish and was sentenced to transportation for fifteen years.

MAY

May Day celebrations at Glatton, 1856.

1 MAY

May Day. A day of celebration and binding of the Maypole and festivities to pray for the continued fertility of the land and good harvests. In some villages 'Jack in the Green', a fellow bedecked in the sprigs of May, would lead a procession through the streets. In other villages across the county May Dolls were often displayed or carried in hoops woven over with May sprigs and ribbons – but beware what May sprigs appear at your door. William Keatinge Clay in his *History of Waterbeach* records the village May Day celebrations of 1820:

> Our May Day was our grandest holiday. Preparatory to its celebration the young men collected materials to form a garland; they consisted or ribands, flowers and silver spoons,

Raising the Maypole in the eighteenth century.

with a silver tankard to suspend in the centre ... Our young men, early in the morning, or rather, late at night, went into the fields to collect the emblems of their esteem or disapprobation; then woe betide the girl of loose habits, the slattern and the scold; for while the young woman who had been foremost in the dance, and whose amiable manners had entitled her to our esteem, had a large branch of whitethorn planted by her cottage door, the girl of loose manners a blackthorn planted by hers, the slattern had an elder tree planted by hers; and the scold a bunch of nettles tied to the latch of her cottage door.

2 MAY 1646

King Charles I came to Little Gidding while on the run after the Battle of Naseby. The King had previously visited the Christian community in the village during the spring of 1642. The religious settlement had been founded by Nicholas Ferrar in 1625 and was significant

King Charles I on his flight after the Battle of Naseby, 1646.

because it was the first Anglican community to be established in the country. Sadly, this visit was not so happy; the King was not far from capture and he had to be guided across the fields by John Ferrar to the safety of Coppingford Lodge. The King continued to flee, but was eventually captured at Southwell in Nottinghamshire on 6 May.

3 MAY Grim Sayings of Cambridgeshire

Over singers, Swavesey ringers,
Bluntisham runners, Earith gunners,
Colne noddles, Somersham suckeggs,
Fenton frogs, Pidley pancakes,
War boys, Wistow lads,
Bury creepheads, Ramsey scabs.

4 MAY John Howard Reports on the Prisons of Cambridgeshire & Huntingdon

Cambridge Town Gaol, 1782:

Below is a room for criminals known as the hole, about 21ft by 7ft. The prisoner, whom I saw there in 1776, was a miserable object; he had been confined some weeks. There was no allowance, the prisoners received relief from several colleges, viz St John's, Trinity, Christ's etc. Above are rooms for debtors and criminals, one of which is called the cage. No court, no water accessible to the prisoners. Clauses against spirituous liquors, and the act for preserving the health of prisoners not hung up. Gaoler no salary, there is a licence for beer.

Thomas Bell, 'The Cambridge Giant'.

5 MAY 1813

Thomas Bell, 'The Cambridge Giant', exhibited himself at the Hog in the Pound, Oxford Street, London. Bell (36) was born to parents of average height and apprenticed to his family craft of blacksmith, but so many people were drawn to come and see him that he relinquished his life in the forge and began exhibiting himself at the principal cities, towns and fairs around the country. Bell stood 7ft 2in high, his hands were 11in long, his middle fingers 6in in length. Curiously, his advertising literature stated he was also 'double jointed'.

6 MAY 1849

Riot at Fen Ditton Church. Edward Smith a local gardener and former sexton, had made comments concerning the chastity of the rector's wife, a woman much younger than her husband, who had worked as the reverend's cook before they married. The rector's wife soon heard of what had been said and brought the matter before the Ecclesiastical Court, then the Court of Arches, which sentenced Smith to do penance and pay costs of £42 7s 6d.

The news of the event spread and gentle folk from Cambridge applied for reserved seats, but they were to be trounced by the many local labourers and lightermen, who filled the church and many more made a rowdy crowd outside. The service commenced with the sermon 'Judge not, that ye be not judged,' but this was met with cat calls and hoots of approbation and laughter. Smith arrived at the church wrapped in the typical white sheet for the penance, but he was met with cheers and could not be heard as he attempted to read his recantation.

Suddenly the church broom was hurled at the church dignitaries. Hassocks were thrown, pews torn up and hurled about the church, and some of the mob started to ring the bells. Smith did finish his speech, but no one really heard it and when he was done he was cheered and carried shoulder high from the church to the Plough Inn. The rector and his wife fled to the rectory, followed by an angry crowd who smashed the windows with anything which came to hand. A great collection was raised to pay Smith's costs, but none of it seems to have reached him – perhaps it was all drunk away on the riotous day. Poor old Smith ended up serving five months' imprisonment in the County Gaol for non-payment of the costs and he was finally discharged as an insolvent debtor.

7 MAY John Howard Reports on the Prisons of Cambridgeshire & Huntingdon

County Bridewell at Cambridge Castle, 1782.

> Keeper, Simon Saunders the County Gaoler is attentive and humane. Situated in the castle yard the bridewell building joins to the gaoler's house. It consists of two work rooms and over them two rooms; one for men with four cages six and a half feet by four and a half and the other for women with two cages. No court, no water accessible to prisoners, only one sewer and that very offensive. There is no allowance, the prisoners have the profit of their work, which is beating hemp and making mops.

8 MAY 1808

Ann 'Nanny', Izzard a 'knowing woman' of Great Paxton, was attacked after being accused of being a witch. On Thursday 5 May Izzard had given advice about loading a wagon to a woman at St Neots Market; the woman ignored the advice and it overturned on her homeward journey. The woman publicly charged Izzard with 'overturning the cart by means of her infernal art, on purpose to spoil her goods.' There was already a suspicion that Izzard was a witch; only the previous month she had been blamed for the illness of three young women and panic spread rapidly across the local community.

On Sunday 8 May the superstitious locals took the matter into their own hands, broke into Izzard's cottage, dragged Ann from her bed and threw her naked into the yard, dashing her head against the stones. Her arms were torn with pins, an allusion to the belief a witch's curse against you can be broken by scratching and drawing the blood of the said witch. She was also beaten to 'drive out the devil' with a large stick she usually used to bar the door. The mob dispersed but returned again the following day, when she was again dragged from her house and 'pricked'. The following day the villagers attempted to 'swim' her, but she fled to the home of Revd Nicholson, who gave her shelter from the mob.

A number of those who assaulted Ann were tried and found guilty, but none of them accepted they had done anything wrong. On 16 October 1809, Izzard was assaulted again by Judith Day (57) and her daughter Elizabeth (34). Izzard brought the two before the magistrate and they were gaoled the following day. Unable to live without scorn and taint of witchcraft at Great Paxton, Nanny Izzard lived out her last years in St Neots, where she was still 'cruelly treated'. She died in January 1838, aged 93.

9 MAY Strange Tales and Folklore of Cambridgeshire: 'Stinking' Stetchworth

'Stinking Stetchworth' was an unfortunate epithet. Perhaps it arose from the nasty contents of the Devil's Ditch, which ran close to the village, but more likely it was due to the poor sanitary conditions it suffered, particularly after one of the lanes which ran off the High Street – which was known for years as 'Turd Alley' because it was where the villagers emptied the buckets from their privies. When the locals saw their chance they did not hesitate to get rid of the stink and the stain on their village's name by becoming one of the first villages in the area to connect to mains sewerage.

10 MAY 1867

Severe thunder storms over the county. At Barrington a farmer's son and five labourers were ploughing in a field when the storm rolled over them at 1 p.m. Taking shelter under a nearby straw stack, a flash of lightening rendered them all insensible. All revived except Mr Patman (56), a man who had loyally served on the farm for about forty years. Patman had taken the majority of the lightening strike and was found to be lifeless, 'his shoes, leggings and hat torn to atoms.' A boy at work in the same field had the upper portion of one of his shoes cut clean out along with a piece of flesh about the size of a shilling, from under his great toe, by the same blast.

11 MAY 1812

Cambridgeshire man assassinates Prime Minister Spencer Percival. Born in St Neots in about 1770, John Bellingham became a merchant broker and export representative. Arrested and imprisoned in Russia after an allegation of fraud, Bellingham was refused assistance from the British Ambassador. The original charges were dropped, but his imprisonment had caused severe debts and he was retained behind bars on charges of bankruptcy.

Killed by a strike of lightening on 10 May.

After a total of almost six years Bellingham was released and he returned to England an embittered man. He wrote numerous letters to politicians and officials explaining his case and seeking compensation, all to no avail. One reply from the Prime Minister's office described Bellingham's claim as groundless. After months of secret preparation, on 11 May Bellingham took his family to an exhibition of paintings and casually remarked he had some business to attend to and proceeded to the lobby entrance of the House of Commons. At 5.15 p.m. Prime Minister Spencer Percival entered; Bellingham calmly walked forward, fired a single shot that penetrated the Prime Minister's heart, and then sat on a bench. The cry went up of 'Where is the murderer?' Bellingham replied, 'I am the unfortunate man.'

Tried on Wednesday 13 May, Bellingham was found guilty and executed in front of Newgate Prison. His body was delivered to the anatomists, his bones boiled clean and prepared for future use by students. His head disappeared a few years later and was only discovered decades later in a box in the cellars of the medical school, some helpful doctor having carefully written 'Bellingham' in ink across the forehead.

12 MAY Punishments of the Past: Cuck Stools and Ducking Stools

There is a good deal of confusion between Cucking and Ducking Stools. Both were widely used for the punishment of minor offences, especially in relation to strumpets and scolds.

John Bellingham.

Bellingham assasinates Prime Minister Spencer Percival.

A portable Ducking Stool.

The Cuck Stool, or Stool of Repentance, was used from before the Norman Conquest. Seated on this stool the woman, her head and feet bare, was publicly exposed at her door or paraded through the streets amidst the jeers of the crowd. Its use declined after the introduction of the Scolds Bridle in the middle of the sixteenth century and disappeared after the introduction of the Ducking Stool.

There is no evidence to suggest Cuck Stools were used for submerging offenders in water: this was the purpose of the Ducking Stool. Used on scolds and strumpets from the sixteenth century, the Ducking Stool was usually made from oak and fixed with heavy iron band to make it sink. When the culprit was fixed in the chair it was lifted by a pole, chain or rope contrivance over the water then lowered and raised accordingly to duck the scold.

In 1745 the Cambridge Sessions ordered the Chief Constable to pay Alderman Pretlove a bill of £1 6s for a Ducking Stool at the great bridge. William Cole (1714–1782), recalled the Cambridge Ducking Stool:

> I remember to have seen a woman ducked for scolding. The chair was hung by a pulley fastened to a beam about the middle of the bridge, in which the woman was confined, and let down three times, and then taken out. The bridge was then of timber ... The ducking stool was constantly hanging in its place, and on the back of it were engraved devils laying hold of scolds. Some time afterwards a new chair was erected in the place of the old one, having the same devices carved upon it, and well painted and ornamented. When the new bridge of stone was erected in 1754 this chair was taken away.

But that was not to be the last chair; that was made in 1766 when the *Cambridge Sessions* recorded:

It is this day agreed and ordered at the request of the Grand Jury that a Ducking Chair be made and put up at the Great Bridge at the expense of the Town of Cambridge, and that the same be suffered to hang there at all times until this court shall otherwise order.

13 MAY Cures of Fenland Cunning Folk: Aches and Pains

If troubled by an ache to the face or in the ear, insert the core of a roasted onion in your ear. If you wish to ward off rheumatism, wear garters made from dried eel skin just above the knee.

Cramp is prevented by wearing a ring made out of gold coffin handles, or by obtaining a 'crampe ringe' blessed by the reigning sovereign. For less affluent folk a quick word with a 'cunning woman' would probably result with the advice to place one's boots or shoes by the bedside in the form of a cross tau, or by keeping a basin of spring water under the bed. Another preventative charm for cramp was to obtain the knee-bone of a sheep or human patella from the local Sexton (the latter considered the most potent) carried in a pocket, nearer the skin the better, or laid under the pillow at night.

14 MAY 1910

George Henry Victor Pilsworth of Cambridge was fined £4 and costs at Huntingdon Police Court for driving a motor car 'at a speed dangerous to the public' at Little Stukeley. Police witnesses put the speed of the car at a startling 26mph!

15 MAY 1837

A man later identified as William Hyde of Peterborough was found in the middle of the road near Seangate Hill, Upton, Huntingdon. His head was so dreadfully crushed, that no features could be distinguished. The body was carried to Upton where his sister-in-law and son identified him from the clothes. An inquest was held. The jury returned a verdict of 'accidental death', by what means they did not conclude, but they believed it was probable the unfortunate man had suffered a fit (a condition he was known to suffer) collapsed to the ground and a mail coach or similar had run over his head.

16 MAY 1913

Suffragette incendiary! Fire breaks out in buildings on Storey's Way, Cambridge. PC Smith was on the scene at 1.05 a.m. on the morning of 17th; one house was ablaze, but just as the fire brigade arrived a second fire was found in another house. Smith noted signs of forced entry and made his way into the house. The staircase was ablaze from top to bottom and in an adjoining compartment there was a ladder, bound round with pink flannelette and stinking of paraffin. More rags and fuel were found around the building and the footprints of a woman were clearly visible in the wet cement of the kitchen floor.

Under the broken window he found a spot of blood and a woman's gold watch. This was traced to Miriam Pratt (23), a school teacher who lodged with her aunt and uncle, a police officer on Turner Road, Norwich. He had recognised it as a gift he had given Miriam about five years ago. Miriam was a Suffragette, and had told them she was going to the East Cambridgeshire election to deliver leaflets and had returned on the evening of Saturday 17 May. When confronted by her uncle, she confessed she had been at Storey's Way and had cut herself as she attempted to get the putty out of the window to remove

GENERAL ELECTION.

To the Electors of Cambridge.

Mark what your PARLIAMENTARY CANDIDATES
say about

WOMEN'S SUFFRAGE

In their Election Addresses.

Borough :

Mr. S. O. BUCKMASTER : "It should also be an essential feature of our policy to establish yet firmer the principle of representative government, and for this purpose to remove the anomalies and inequalities of our present electoral system. As part of such reform it is to my mind just and for the general good that **women, who now share the burdens, should also share the responsibilities of the State.**"

Mr. ALMERIC PAGET : "While doubting if the majority of the women of this country yet desire such a change, **I am prepared, when the question arises, to support a Measure which will extend the Suffrage by removing the disqualification of sex.**"

West Cambridgeshire :

The Hon. E. S. MONTAGU : "I hope that in the new Parliament the Liberal Government . . . will carry out **the reform of our Electoral and Franchise Systems, including . . . the Enfranchisement of Women.**"

East Cambridgeshire (Newmarket Division)

Sir CHARLES D. ROSE : "I would support a measure for the Parliamentary Enfranchisement of Women."

Support the Suffragettes! A Cambridge election handbill of 1910.

the pane. She said she was with two other women, one she named as Miss Markham, the other she refused to name. Miriam Pratt was insistent she was not the one who had started the fire.

At Cambridge Assizes Miriam's uncle gave evidence against her. Found guilty of arson, Mr Justice Bray sentenced Pratt to eighteen months. She was not forgotten: the Suffragette press extolled her sacrifice and cause. In October 1913, Mr Justice Bray, with the Corporation and local Magistracy, attended service at Norwich Cathedral. During the Collect a group of Suffragists rose and chanted the words, 'Lord help and save Miriam Pratt and all those being tortured in prison for conscience sake.' Having finished their recital the Suffragists resumed their seats. They were not asked to leave the building and distributed printed accounts of Miss Pratt's defence at the cathedral doors after the service.

17 MAY 1819

Mary Ann Weems (21) was murdered by her husband, Thomas Weems. Before burial of this poor girl, her body was displayed in the White Hart pub. The epitaph on her memorial stone in the churchyard of St Mary the Virgin, Godmanchster, reads:

> As a warning
> To the young of both sexes
> This stone is erected by public Subscription
> over the remains of MARY ANN WEEMS
> who at an early age became acquainted
> with THOMAS WEEMS formerly of this Parish
> this connextion terminating in a compulsory
> Marriage occasioned him soon to desert her
> and wishing to be Married to another Woman
> he filled up the measure of his iniquity
> by resolving to murder his Wife
> which he barbarously perpetrated at Wendy
> on their Journey to London toward which place
> he had induced her to go under the mask
> of reconciliation May the 7th 1819
> He was taken within a few hours after
> the crime was committed, tried and
> subsequently executed at Cambridge
> on the 7th of August in the same Year
> Ere Crime you perpetrate survey this Stone
> Learn hence the God of Justice sleeps not on his Throne
> But marks the Sinner with unerring Eye
> The suffering Victim hears and makes the Guilty die.

Weems was actually executed on 6 August (see that date for what happened to his body).

18 MAY 1846

Clearing up continues after the previous day's fire at Huntingdon Union Workhouse. The fire was caused by a factory inmate named Ann Peacock (20), a woman who had already been punished twenty times in the union for violence and insubordination. She had been ordered to clear out a bedroom, but soon the alarm of 'fire!' was raised by another inmate. The union officers burst into the room and found Peacock quietly watching four beds as they burned; she had thrown hot coals upon them and more coals were strewn over the floor. When questioned why she had done this, she arrogantly replied, 'Oh, I told you I would do it when you stopped my dinner yesterday.' At the assizes she was found guilty of arson and sentenced to death, accompanied by an intimation that it would be commuted to a short term of transportation.

19 MAY 1848

Smallpox prevalent in the county. At Littleport alone over 200 people were infected; for many this dreadful disease proved to be fatal.

As a Warning
to the Young of both Sexes
This Stone is erected by public Subscription
over the remains of MARY ANN WEEMS.
who at an early age became acquainted
with THOMAS WEEMS formerly of this Parish
this connexion terminating in a compulsory
Marriage occasioned him soon to desert her
and wishing to be Married to another Woman
he filled up the measure of his iniquity
by resolving to murder his Wife
which he barbarously perpetrated at Wendy
on their Journey to London toward which place
he had induced her to go under the mask
of reconciliation May the 7ᵗʰ 1819
He was taken within a few hours after
the crime was committed tried and
subsequently executed at Cambridge
on the 7ᵗʰ of August in the same Year

Ere Crime you perpetrate survey this Stone
Learn hence the God of Justice sleeps not on his throne
But marks the Sinner with unerring Eye
The suffering Victim hears and makes the cause his own

The memorial stone for Mary Ann Weems in the churchyard of St Mary the Virgin, Godmanchester.

The original grave marker stone for the body of Mary Ann Weems.

20 MAY 1864

John Clare dies. Born in Helpston in the soke of Peterborough, Clare attended the school in Glinton Church until he was twelve and declared his love for Mary Joyce by carving her initials on the external stonework of the east wall, but their love was forbidden. Clare, an agricultural labourer, was not seen as a worthy suitor by Mary's parents. The couple met illicitly many times and he began to write poetry, which attracted great acclaim and was widely published, but by the time his success came he had married another.

John Clare was a troubled man, he was always torn between his literary life in London and his family back in the country and he began to suffer severe depression. His final and best work, *Rural Muse*, was published in 1835, but soon after, between 1837 and 1841, Clare was in an asylum. Clare left the asylum to walk home to Helpston in the belief he was to be reunited with his first love Mary Joyce, he had grown confused and believed he was married to Mary. When he arrived Clare would not believe Mary's family when they told him Mary had died three years earlier. John Clare was committed to the Northampton General Lunatic Asylum, where he remained for the rest of his life.

21 MAY 1731

Destructive fire at Great Whyte. Most of the High Street was destroyed when fire tore through all the houses from the School House to the High Bridge. Eighty houses, shops, granaries, barns and outhouses were destroyed, and along with them a great quantity of malt and flour.

22 MAY 1816

The Littleport Riot. Times were hard and wages were low, and in many rural areas labourers gathered to create mutual benefit societies. The Littleport club met at the Globe on the evening of 22 May 1816, so many were found in need that, bad feelings ran high. A man named Cornwall sought out a powerful horn and soon a crowd of several hundred people followed him back to the Globe pub, the men armed themselves with a motley array of farm implements and a few guns and took to the streets. Shops were attacked, windows smashed and some local people were intimidated, houses entered and looted and other properties wrecked. With their blood up and buoyed with foolish confidence the rioters decided to proceed to Ely.

Revd John Vachell, vicar of Littleport and town magistrate, had fled with his family to Ely after the vicarage had been attacked earlier that evening. He raised the alarm with fellow clergymen magistrates, Revd William Metcalfe and Revd Sir Henry Bate Dudley. Thomas Archer was sent as messenger to Bury St Edmunds to summon the First Dragoon Guards and many tradesmen of Ely were called up and sworn in as emergency special constables. Between and 5 and 6 a.m. on 23 May the rioters arrived at Ely. Revd Metcalfe immediately read out the Riot Act and asked what they wanted. The reply were cries of 'the price of a stone of flour per day' and 'our children are starving, give us a living wage.' Metcalfe said they would have it, but he said he would consult with the other magistrates and advised the rioters to return to Littleport. The rioters marched on; Metcalfe requested they proceed to the Market Place, most did and they were joined by many Ely residents.

The magistrates retired to the White Hart, drafted a written agreement and most rioters were satisfied. To celebrate their relief at concluding the riot the magistrates gave out free beer. The result was that drink fuelled instances of violence and robbery now flared against the wealthy traders and the affluent across Ely.

The arrival of the Dragoons was enough to restore order. The following day the Dragoons, joined by the Royston Troop of Volunteer Cavalry, proceeded to Littleport with Henry Bate Dudley and John Bacon, a Bow Street Constable. The main body of the rioters had barricaded themselves in the George & Dragon pub. After a brief but bloody exchange the rioters within were taken, more were arrested across the Fens; in all eighty people were brought under arrest to Ely. At the assizes, before Mr Justice Abbot, Mr Justice Burrough and Mr Edward Christian, the trial of the Littleport rioters lasted for six days and at the conclusion the death sentence was passed on twenty-four of them. There was a public outcry and the capital sentences were readdressed; nine were transported, most received a year in Ely gaol, but five were still to hang.

On Friday 28 June 1816, William Beamis, George Crow, John Dennis, Isaac Harley and Thomas South were executed on the gallows at Ely. Once they had swung for the approved time the bodies were taken down and removed for display at a cottage on Goal Street. They were buried the following day in St Mary's churchyard and a stone plaque was erected at the side of the tower to their memory and as 'a warning to others.'

23 MAY 1905

Rumours spread that the Great North Road in the county of Huntingdon was 'sown' with hobnails; pieces of files and assorted dangerous metals that could cause accidents. When stories of an elderly man named William Hayes being found badly injured after being knocked down on the Great North Road between Buckden and St the Huntingdon appeared in the press, the Chief Constable was quick to write to *The Times* to condemn the scaremongering, pointing out a man had been injured, a car had passed him, but he had not stated the man had been knocked down by a motorcar and 'so far there is no evidence that such was the case.'

Hundred of Ely, In the Isle of Ely.

The **MAGISTRATES** agree, and do Order, that the **OVERSEERS** shall pay to each poor Family Two **SHILLINGS** per Head per Week, when **FLOUR** is Half-a-Crown a Stone, such Allowance be raised in Proportion when the Price of Flour is higher, and that the Price of Labour shall be Two Shillings per Day, whether Married or Single, and that the Labourer shall be paid his full Wages by the Farmer who Hires him.

No Person to be prosecuted for any thing that has been done to the present Time; provided that every **MAN** immediately returns peaceably to his own Home.

ELY, May 23, 1816.

The printed bill of the magistrates' promise to the Littleport Rioters.

The memorial at St Mary's Church, Ely, to those executed for their part in the Littleport Riots, 1816.

SCENE of Fatal Motor Car Accident at Abington. M⋯

Even the most sleepy of Cambridgshire roads were liable to death and disaster in the early years of motoring.

24 MAY 1811

After being crossed in love, Elizabeth James of Peterborough took her own life with poison. Suicides were not permitted to be interred in consecrated ground (*see* 23 December) and thus she was buried in the road leading to Spalding. Relations of the unfortunate girl erected a stone nearby, inscribed, 'Near this spot were deposited, on 24th May 1811, the sad remains of Elizabeth James; an awful momento against the horrid crime of suicide – Passenger! Take warning: you see here a fatal instance of human weakness and the dreadful consequence of misplaced affection.'

25 MAY 1822

Advertisements appear in newspapers and flyers claiming 'Zachariah Whitmore of Philadelphia, North America, begs to inform the inhabitants of Cambridge that he intends starting from Lynn on his water Velocipede at 12 o'clock and will arrive at Cambridge between 6 and 7 o'clock in the evening on Whit Monday next.' About 2,000 people assembled on the banks of the Cam on 27 May to observe the feat, only to discover, after several hours wait, it was all a hoax.

26 MAY Tales from the Gaols: Oakum Picking

Oakum picking was a common occupation set for prisoners during the nineteenth century. The process could be carried out in solitary confinement cells or with other prisoners, in silence, in workrooms or oakum sheds. The prisoner was given a weighed length of old ships' rope, often black with tar and deeply engrained with salt. After separating the rope into its corkscrewed, coils these would then be unrolled by sliding them back and

Another invention to enable the Fen man to walk on water.

forth on the knee with the palm of the hand until the meshes were loosened. The strands were then separated and cleaned of the salt and tar on them. This 'stuff' was used for caulking the seams in the sides and decks of wooden ships. Men, women and children prisoners all picked oakum; it was very hard on the fingers, and rope cuts were common, as were blisters, which proved very painful until hands hardened to the work. Prisoners were expected to produce 3–4lb every two hours; shifts of oakum picking could last up to twelve hours. The prisoners were paid for this labour; on average young offenders could earn up to 17*s* a year for picking oakum – literally money for old rope!

27 MAY 1774

The Cambridgeshire Militia, under the command of their colonel, Lord Montfort, made a fixed bayonet attack upon some of the scholars of Cambridge, several of whom were wounded. Similar scenes took place the next day. To prevent such collisions, the militia were removed the following year to Wisbech, Ely, March, Downham and Littleport.

The Peterborough Sessions House, c. 1905.

28 MAY 1932

The Tebbutt family were found shot dead at Meads End, Cambridge. The family and staff had been planning to go on holiday, Mr Herbert Tebbutt (46) was ready, but his 'wife' Helen Williams (38) was not. Tebbutt sent the servant girls out to wait in the car, but after a short wait they heard pistol shots from inside the house. Rushing inside, a horrific crime scene lay in front of them. Herbert and Helen lay dead in the hall near the telephone. Helen's daughter from a previous marriage, Betty (12), lay in the kitchen where their sons Michael (2) and Dickie (18 months) were also found in their perambulators. All of them had been shot: a German automatic pistol was found clasped in Tebbutt's hand. At the inquest it was revealed that Tebbutt had divorced his wife in 1929, and Williams had been named as co-repondent and moved into the Tebbutt house soon after. Herbert Tebbutt hated paying alimony; he could afford to pay, but despised handing over the money and had built up arrears. The coroner was in no doubt the divorce and its cost implications 'played upon Tebbutt's mind' and, combined with his 'uncertain' temper, the jury returned a verdict of 'wilful murder' of his family followed by suicide 'while temporarily insane.'

29 MAY Punishments of the Past: The Peterborough Quarter Sessions

A little-known fact was that under an ancient charter, the Peterborough Bench had the assize power of oyer and terminer or general gaol delivery and thus its chairman could pass the death sentence, a privilege extended to only one other, that of the Bench of magistrates at Lancaster.

30 MAY 1814

The Treaty of Paris heralds the end of the Napoleonic Wars (for the time being) and the end of the detention camp for French soldiers and sailors who were prisoners of war at Norman Cross. Built in the late 1790s to hold between 5–6,000 prisoners, the site was surrounded by a perimeter fence and ditch and then divided into four quadrants, each containing two four-storey prison blocks that housed up to 500 men sleeping in hammocks. Two regiments of soldiers were stationed in the barracks to guard the prisoners. It was known for the site to house over 7,000 men.

By 1801 the conditions in which the prisoners were held had become a matter of public concern; they had insufficient clothing and instances of sickness, such as fever, consumption, dysentery and typhus were often rife; there were a handful of escapes and in 1804 it was discovered the prisoners had been involved in forgery after printing plates and related implements were discovered. With some prisoners in a state of near nakedness, the British Government provided them with prison uniforms of sulphur yellow colour in the hope these easily-identified clothes would prevent further escapes. When peace with France was declared in 1814 the local people, camp guards and the prisoners joined together for the celebrations, all prisoners had left the garrison by June and by June 1816 most of the prison buildings were finally demolished. A total of 1,770 French prisoners of war had died here over their years of captivity, but it was only on 28 July 1914 that memorial was erected to their memory and the mark *L'Entente Cordial*.

31 MAY 1849

Inquest at Fulbourne on view of the body of John Nichol Luxmoore, a student of St John's college. Luxmoore had been riding with his friend, Mr Stuart of Trinity, when he proposed a race along the old Roman road outside Babraham towards Cambridge. The horses galloped, Stuart took the lead, but turning around to see where his friend was saw him lying on his back upon the ground. Rushing to his friends' aid, Stuart found him unconscious; he died a few minutes later. Post-mortem examination revealed he had landed on his head. The jury returned a verdict of 'death through an accidental fall from his horse.'

JUNE

A Witch Bottle. All manner of curious charms were tried to ward off any malign attention from witches. Among those judged most effective were 'witch bottles', 'witch jugs' or 'witch jars'. Salt-glazed 'Bellarmine' jugs were often used, so nicknamed after Cardinal Robert Bellarmine (1542–1621), who was said to look like the grimacing face on the side that kept away evil; inside there would often be a potent mix of thorns, iron pins or horseshoe nails, finger and toe nail parings, urine and hair from every member of the family, the belief being that if a witch sent a curse to your house, when it came down the chimney it would magically be drawn into the bottle and away from the family members who had been cursed. This example, displayed at the Norris Museum in Huntingdon, was found to still contain the iron pins of the charm in the neck of the bottle when it was discovered under the hearth of a seventeenth-century cottage at Wennington.

1 JUNE Cures of Fenland Cunning Folk: Inoculations

With so many Fen families reliant on the tried and trusted 'cures' of the local cunning folk, more 'modern' medicine was often met with suspicion and sometimes violence. In 1768 two philanthropic gentlemen named Sutton and Bond opened a house for inoculations at Yaxley. A mob of locals soon rose up, completely demolished the building and compelled its human inmates, after shooting one in the arm, to save their lives by flight.

2 JUNE 1944

Soham railway station was destroyed when an ammunition train caught fire. Further disaster was averted through the gallantry of the driver, Ben Gimbert, and fireman James Nightall. Gimbert had spotted that the front wagon had caught fire as they approached Soham. Bringing the train to a halt, Nightall uncoupled the blazing wagon and Gimbert returned with the engine to tow the blazing wagon out of the town and away from the rest of the train. He towed it about 140yds forward into the station, then slowed down to shout to the signalman, Frank 'Sailor' Bridges, who was waiting on that offside platform with a full fire bucket hoping to douse the flames. Suddenly the blazing wagon went up in one massive blast, sending Bridges to the floor mortally wounded.

The station was to reduced rubble and a crater 60ft wide and 15ft deep was caused by the blast. More than 500 homes and twenty-two other buildings were damaged, but if it had not been for the gallant action of Gimbert and Nightall the whole town could have been destroyed. Both men received the George Cross. Ben Gimbert had been blown clear by some 200yds and was badly injured, but James Nightall had been killed outright and the train's guard, Herbert Clarke, was severely shocked.

3 JUNE 1930

Double murder and suicide at King's College. Douglas Newton Potts, although a promising student, lived a Walter Mitty existence; he was extravagant, dressed in eccentric clothes and told the people at the hostelries he patronised that he was a prince. Potts actually came from a modest background, but he soon got himself into debt and found reality was creeping up on him.

Potts and another student ran a scam ripping off Cambridge tailors; when one would not play along, Potts produced a pistol, he did not directly threaten, but the message was clear. The police were informed and the boys thought they had better get out of town for a while. When Potts returned, his tutor, Mr Alexander Wollaston, sent for him to explain his absence. In an unfortunate turn of events shortly after Potts arrived in his tutor's office Detective Sergeant Francis Willis arrived unexpectedly, Potts thought he had been set up and several gunshots were heard from inside the office.

Potts shot Mr Wollaston three times in the upper body; he died soon after. Detective Sergeant Willis, who had thrown himself at Potts, had been hit twice, once in the shoulder and once in the groin was seriously wounded. Potts then turned the gun on himself, discharging a shot to his head; he died shortly after. The path of the second bullet inside Detective Sergeant Willis had caused extensive internal injuries. Rushed to Addenbrooke's Hospital, he was given an emergency operation, but died in the early hours of 4 June.

4 JUNE 1863

The Town of Cambridge Association for the prosecution of felons displayed posters seeking 'A COMMON SWINDLER', who had claimed to be Charles Wickes of the Woodlands, Spring Grove and the Carlton Club of Pall Mall, London who had obtained a sum of money and several valuable articles under false pretences from two members of the Association, a warrant was issued for his apprehension. He was described as being about 36 years old, 5ft 9in high 'having light brown hair and whiskers, small light green eyes (inflamed from intemperate habits), fresh complexion, full face, stoutly built and broad chest.' Those with information could contact Mr W.G. Turrall, Superintendent of Cambridge Police. If the information led to Wickes', conviction the informant was assured he would be 'rewarded for his trouble and all reasonable expenses paid.'

5 JUNE 1940

A loss to both worlds. Brilliant research scientist Oliver Gatty of Grantchester and engineer Alfred Chessum were fatally burned during an ARP experiment. The inquest at Cambridge returned a verdict of 'death by misadventure'. Gatty's great interest had been in electrically charged surfaces. His imagination, fuelled with the potential and applications of this, led to him studying the role such surfaces played in biological phenomena. His obituary also pointed out he had also 'made a patient and critical study of a variety of allegedly supernatural manifestations.'

6 JUNE 1648

The siege breaks at Woodcroft Castle. Michael Hudson, doctor of divinity and chaplain to Charles I, was one of the King's most loyal servants. Imprisoned when Charles was incarcerated on the Isle of Wight, he escaped, was recaptured and sent to the Tower, but escaped again. During the renewed fighting in 1648, Hudson raised a troop and made a valiant stand at Woodcroft Castle, where they were attacked by Parliamentary troops led by Colonel Woodhead. The colonel's brother-in-law had been killed in the first attack; the enraged colonel led the second assault personally and breached the defences. According to the seventeenth-century Royalist historian Anthony Wood, Hudson and his men fought vigorously from the battlements, but 'on promise of quarter they yielded,' but no mercy was offered to Hudson, who was flung off the tower. As he fell he managed to catch hold of 'a spout or outstone' and clung on. One of the Roundheads callously chopped off Hudson's hands at the wrist, causing him to fall into the moat, but he did not die in the process. He struggled out of the moat, wrists spurting blood, to be met by more Roundheads. He begged piteously for help, but was silenced when one of them cut out his tongue; another delivered the coup de grace with the butt of his rifle. These two soldiers directly involved in the final killing of Dr Hudson were cursed men; one died in agony after his gun blew up, the other, who displayed the tongue he cut out as a grim exhibit in a travelling show, died in abject poverty. The horrible demise of Dr Hudson is said to have be re-enacted in spectral form on this day ever since.

7 JUNE The Prisons of Cambridgeshire & Huntingdon

Table of Fees to be levied upon prisoners, by direction of the Lord Bishop of Ely 1794:

For the board of each prisoner when he diets with the Gaoler   4s
For room and bed furnished by the Gaoler per week:-

Straw Bedding	1s
Plank with bedding (otherwise you sleep on the floor)	1s 6d
For room and bed furnished by the Gaoler (an iron bed with sheets)	2s
Discharge fee to be paid by each Debtor	16s 8d
Gaoler's garnish to be paid by all arrivals	1s 4d

8 JUNE 1916

Harriet Blewitt, a woman who had failed to appear at Peterborough Sessions on a charge of stealing six Treasury notes three weeks previously, was found in a well near her house.

9 JUNE 1874

The Cambridge Improvement Commissioners considered Dr Buchanan's report on the recent outbreak of enteric fever at Gonville and Caius College. The report stated: 'In the town of Cambridge, since midsummer last, enteric fever has been more than usually prevalent. In July and August deaths occurred and in October the disease became still more prevalent and fatal, especially in the neighbourhood of Barnwell.' Having dwelt at length upon the causes of the deaths at Caius College he concluded, after his recent visit that he 'found the means of ventilation were apparently efficient and safe and that structural changes had been made by which it will in future be impossible for drinking water to become impregnated with sewer air.'

10 JUNE 1905

After the 'May' races there was a sudden rush to cross to the towpath and the flat-bottomed ferry *Red Grind*, attached to the Plough Inn on the boat race course below Cambridge, was filled to the degree Councillor Wallis was convinced it would sink and advised his friends not to go on. As the ferry got to about mid-stream it 'turned turtle' and about twenty passengers were thrown into the water. A number of young men dived in to rescue those who were struggling. A woman from Bishop Stortford was revived by artificial respiration, but she died later. Two other ladies were brought out of the river dead; a Mrs Thompson of Malta Road, and Miss Murkin of Selwyn Terrace, Newnham, who was to have wed the following Monday.

11 JUNE 1892

Inquest held at the Pike and Eel, Old Chesterton, on the body of Christ's College undergraduate Mr H.C.L. Lovett (21), who had been struck dead by lightening the previous afternoon. He had been walking to the boat races when there was a sudden flash of lightening and a crash of thunder. His companion, fellow undergraduate Mr Goodman, turned round to see his friend 'stretched flat on his back and quite lifeless.' Dr Keene explained the lightening had struck Mr Lovett at the back of the neck and gave the cause of death as 'concussion of the spinal marrow.' The jury returned a verdict in accordance with the medical evidence.

12 JUNE 1782 John Howard Reports on the Prisons of Cambridgeshire & Huntingdon

Cambridge Town Bridewell:

> The Bridewell stands in the back yard of the keeper's house which was bought and endowed for the encouragement of wool-combers and spinners of Cambridge. The basis of the institution was a legacy from the famous carrier Thomas Hobson. To answer the intention the keeper appointed is a wool-comber. He employs not only several hands upon the foundation of the charity, but many others, among them his prisoners, his salary is paid out of the charity. On the ground floor is one room for men 21ft by 6ft and two lodging rooms for women 9ft 5ft. In these are lately put bedsteads for straw or coverlets. There is a dungeon or dark room for the refractory. Above is a work room 19ft square for women. In the spring of 1779, seventeen women were confined in the day time, and some of them at night, in this room which has no fire place or sewer. This made it extremely offensive and occasioned a fever or sickness among them which alarmed the vice chancellor who ordered all of them to be discharged. Two or three died within a few days. There are now added two rooms in one of which are five cages about 7ft square. There is a small court but no water.
>
> The Vice-chancellor's prisoners have four pence on a Sunday, to prevent the necessity of their working on that day. Those of them that are ill have three pence a day. There is no allowance of bread for town prisoners. Keeper's salary £30, no fees, straw cost £1 1s a year.

13 JUNE 1905

Inspector Drew of Vine Street police station in London arrests Albert Chapman (a native of Cambridge), formerly employed as a night watchman at Grosvenor House. Chapman had offered some jewellery to a pawnbroker on Clapham Park Road, who had recognised it as stolen. Armed with information from Chapman, Drew travelled to Cambridge, where he was met on the station by Mr Holland the Chief Constable and members of the detective and uniform force. They proceeded to Priory Road, where they arrested George White, a tailor.

Upon information supplied by him, they proceeded to a field on the Newmarket Road, where they unearthed jewellery valued at £8,000 that had been stolen from the Duchess of Westminster in May. Tried at the Old Bailey, White was found not guilty; the jewels had been sent in a parcel to him, but he had played no part in the robbery, and had buried them in the field because he had got frightened. Chapman was found guilty of the theft and sentenced to eighteen months with hard labour.

14 JUNE 1910

Execution of James Henry Hancock (55) at the County Gaol, Cambridge. Hancock had come to Old Chesterton in 1894 and worked as a labourer at the sewage works. He met Eliza Marshall soon after his arrival and they were soon living together as common-law man and wife. He gave up the labouring and became a coal hawker. Their relationship deteriorated over the years, to the degree that, by 1910, the violent arguments that erupted saw Eliza being driven to seek the protection of her brother, Alfred Doggett, on a number of occasions. On 4 March 1910, Hancock and Doggett fought and Dogget ended up stabbed. Hancock wandered onto the street and gave himself up. Found guilty and sentenced to death, he was executed by Henry Pierrepoint.

15 JUNE 1757

A mob, chiefly made up of women, assembled at Cambridge, broke open a storehouse in which were lodged about 15 quarters of wheat, the property of a farmer, who had that day refused 9s 6d a bushel for it, and carried it all off. The major was caused to read the Riot Act but before the hour was expired, the mischief was done and the mob dispersed. The following day the mob assembled again having heard twenty-seven sacks of flour were lodged at Small-bridges and, notwithstanding the constables attended, began to assault the place. After a vigorous resistance in which seven or eight were dreadfully wounded, they got to the sacks and carried them off in triumph.

16 JUNE Strange tales and folklore of Cambridgeshire: Quy Church

The villages of Stow and Quy have been joined for centuries, but once they were two settlements and Quy had its own church dedicated to St Nicholas. Incumbents were appointed from 1292 to 1349 while Stow Church was being rebuilt. It was then thought to have reverted to a private chapel for Quy Hall and fell into ruin after the Dissolution. Local folklore likes to explain such happenings and over the years the tale grew up that when the people of Quy wanted to build a church, their day's labours were always destroyed by the Devil at night and in the end they gave up and left the ruins!

17 JUNE 1878

Prisoner John Jones conducts an ingenious escape from Cambridge County Prison. To ensure he covered his tracks, he first broke off a lock to a store room and obtained a civilian suit of clothes, which he hid in his cell. That night, when all were in their cells, he worked loose some of the bricks in his cell and, having made a hole, was able to enter the top corridor. He then let himself down onto the road and disappeared into the night.

18 JUNE 1815

Victory at the Battle of Waterloo. After the battle, Napoleon's magnificent charger Marengo; an iron-grey Arab stallion, was captured, brought to Britain and eventually displayed at the Waterloo Rooms in Pall Mall. Marengo was marvelled at by thousands of visitors and when he was seen at military reviews and parades people were fascinated by the visible scars of five battle wounds and the bullet permanently lodged in his tail, but they were also amazed that such a good tempered, small horse (only 14.1 hands) could have carried the infamous leader Napoleon – but then Napoleon was no giant, he stood 5ft 6.5in tall. Marengo was later sold and went to stud at New Barns near Ely.

After Marengo died aged 38 in 1832, his hide, with its distinctive 'N' brand, ended up stuffed and put on display in Paris while his skeleton was sent to the London Hospital, where it was articulated by Surgeon Wilmott and put on display at the Royal United Service Institution Museum (the skeleton is now on display at the National Army Museum, Chelsea). Marengo's hooves were removed and turned into snuffboxes; one plays a daily role amongst the regimental silver at St James Palace, London. Each day the Captain of the Guard, lunches in the Officer's Mess with the hoof in front of him. On the silver-hinged lid are the words: 'Hoof of Marengo, Barb charger of Napoleon, ridden by him at Marengo, Austerlitz, Jena, Wagram, in the campaign of Russia and lastly, Waterloo.'

A Turn 14,500 times
  Pick 11oz oakum
      per day

B Turn 12,500 times
  Pick 6oz oakum
      per day.

C Turn 10,500 times
      per day.

*A prisoner set
to the crank.*

19 JUNE Tales from the Gaols: The Crank

The Crank was a widely adopted means of occupying refractory prisoners in their solitary cells during the latter half of the nineteenth century. Operated by a single prisoner, the Crank comprised a drum on a metal pillar or a handle set into a wall with a dial to register the number of times the crank handle had been turned – usually about 20 times a minute, a typical target being a total of 10,000 revolutions in eight and a half hours. If the target was not achieved in time the prisoner was given no food until the dial registered the required total. A legacy of the crank remains today; if the prisoner found this task too easy the prison warder would come and tighten the screw making the handle harder to turn, hence the prisoner parlance for warder has, for generations, been 'the screw'.

2 0 JUNE Report of the Prison Inspectors

Huntingdon Gaol and House of Correction 1853. Number of Prisoners at time of Inspection: fifty-four males, seven females and three debtors

There has been no alteration to the buildings or the discipline of the prison since the last inspection. There is still very little industrial employment and the prisoners continue to pass far too much time in bed. There is still no regularly appointed schoolmaster, but the prisoners are instructed by one of the turnkeys ... One prisoner made a complaint. I communicated with a visiting justice and on inquiry found it to be groundless. I find the practice of sorting oats still carried on in this prison, though it is generally confined to those prisoners who misconduct themselves. The Governor in a great measure attributed the decrease in the number of re-committals to this employment, as prisoners re-committed were formerly so employed. I expressed my opinion that the decrease may rather be traced to 'separate confinement'; and I strongly recommend that some industrial employment should be substituted both for sorting oats and crank labour. There are three cranks in the prison; two were in female cells and I found they had been used occasionally by female prisoners. On my recommendation they were at once removed. The number of punishments were great; generally 'supper stopped' for idleness in not performing the appointed task.

    The books and accounts are properly kept. The estimated value of work done for the prison was £4 10s 9d. There was no work done for sale. The daily cost of the food was 4d per head; the net cost per prisoner last year was £24 6s 6d.

2 1 JUNE 1763 Grim Tales of Cambridgeshire: The Coffee House

The following advertisement appeared for a new coffee room which opened next to Emmanuel College:

For the entertainment of such Gentlemen as are desirous of mixing innocent amusement with useful knowledge ... vain glory, impotency, lust and avarice in old age will in their turns be properly exposed and dissected ... squeaking fribble or the cruel, surly, office-bearing tyrant's company is not desired unless duly prepared to see their Foibles exposed in a mirror, in order to prune, lop and divest them of their most odious and obnoxious incumberances, which shall not be sawed, but taken off by a new devised amputation. None but the free, generous, debonnaire and gay are desired to attend.

The coffee house was furnished with prints, drawings and emblematical devices which encouraged innocency and virtue by exposing vice and folly of intemperance and the ill effects of lust – all of which could be enjoyed with coffee or perhaps 'harmless tea, Lacedemonian Broth and invigorating Chocolate, comforting cakes with cooling tarts and jellies,' but no spirituous liquors – Enjoy!

2 2 JUNE 1840

The return of the Littleport stocks. These 'engines of punishment' had been kept at Ely for the punishment of minor offences in this division of the Isle, but the Littleport constable considered the punishment would have a better effect if it was meted out where the offence was committed, so permission was obtained to have them returned. The three young men placed in them for six hours each as punishment for being drunk and disorderly were surely delighted.

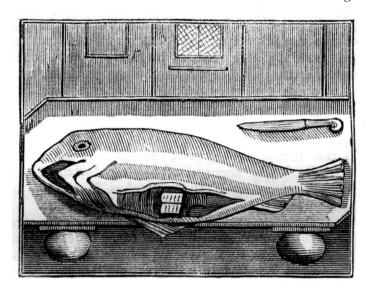

The 'Book Fish' found at Cambridge market, 1626.

23 JUNE 1626

A cod-fish caught off King's Lynn was brought to a fish woman's stall on Cambridge market. When opened it was found to contain a book in its stomach. It was much soiled, and covered in slime, though it had been wrapped in a piece of sailcloth. The book was a duodecimo work written by one John Frith, comprising several treatises on religious subjects. Mr Mead from Christchurch College saw the fish, talked to witnesses and was convinced there had been 'no imposture'. He commented that the find was made all the more curious because Frith had written the treatises while he was confined as a prisoner in a fish cellar at Oxford.

24 JUNE 679

Ely mourns St Etheldreda, foundress and abbess of the monastery at Ely, who died the previous day. In the ninth century it was suggested by the Bishop of Ely that Withburga, her sainted sister, foundress of the nunnery and church at Dereham, should lay with her sisters in Ely, but all at Dereham were vehemently against this. Ely monks gave a great feast to the men of Dereham, but afterwards crept away, broke into Withburga's shrine, loaded the coffin onto an ox-wagon and set off for Ely.

The desecration of the tomb was discovered the following morning. The men of Dereham set off in pursuit and caught up with the monks and the coffin aboard a barge sailing to Ely. The *Liber Eliensis* account states: 'the men of Dereham ran along the bank, throwing clods of earth,' but all to no avail. When the Dereham men returned to the town they found the empty tomb had filled with a spring of clear water, a sign of recompense for their lost saint. The well in the churchyard has never run dry and can still be seen today.

25 JUNE 1842

William Haslop left the Cambridge Pot Fair with a female friend to stroll in the moonlight along the banks of the Cam. They were passed by a group of three men

An eighteenth-century satirical cartoon of the Cambridge Pot Fair.

who suddenly rushed back, tripped up Haslops, then, covering his mouth and eyes, they rifled through his pockets removing the 7 shillings he had about him. Haslop's female companion ran off screaming 'Murder!' The ruffians removed the cash and made off, one of them leaping a hedge into a private garden that turned out to have had no thoroughfare and he fell into the arms of a constable. Brought before the County Assizes, William Freeman was charged with assault and stealing on the Queen's Highway. Feebly attempting to plead he was not involved, Freeman was found guilty and sentenced to six months' hard labour.

26 JUNE 1866

Mr Dodson, a Swavesey harness maker and smallholder, came down for breakfast with his wife and several children at 7 a.m., took his meal out to the field and, with his apprentice, proceeded to his work; all seemed like a normal weekday morning. About 9 a.m. the apprentice visited the back yard, where he was horrified to discover the bodies of Mrs Dodson and the youngest child suspended from a beam in a cow shed. He raised the alarm, Mr Dodson, neighbours and medical assistance were all sent for, but the pair could not be revived.

It was suggested Mrs Dodson may have become unbalanced due to the stress of grief of Mr Dodson losing several beasts in a recent cattle plague. which had been first detected at their smallholding and had spread to other farms in the locality.

The treadmill was designed by William Cubitt.

27 JUNE Tales from the Gaols: The Treadmill

The treadmill was invented by Suffolk engineer and iron founder, William Cubitt. The first was installed at Brixton Prison in 1821 for the grand sum of £6,913 3s 6d. The principal of the treadmill was simple. Looking like an elongated mill wheel, each wheel contained twenty-four steps set eight inches apart, so the circumference of the cylinder was 16ft. The wheel, under the power of the convicts walking up its 'steps' revolved twice in a minute, with a mechanism set to ring a bell on every thirtieth revolution to announce the spell of work was finished. Every man put to labour at the wheel worked fifteen quarter-hour sessions, climbing up to 19,000ft every day. Some mills had purposes and were used to grind corn or pump water, but most drove nothing and the labour of the prisoners was to no avail. In 1895 there were thirty-nine treadmills and twenty-nine cranks in use in British prisons. Treadmills were finally banned by an Act of Parliament in 1898.

28 JUNE 1898

Execution of William Horsford (26). Despite being a newly married man, Horsford, a farmer from Spaldwick, carried on his affair with his cousin, Mrs Annie Holmes (38) of St Neots. He had intended to stop the liaisons, but in December 1897 she informed him she was pregnant, and with that she sealed her fate. Horsford went to a chemist in Thrapstone and bought ninety grains of strychnine 'to kill rats'.

On 7 January 1898, Annie was expecting a visit from Horsford, but instead she received a letter. She had been feeling unwell most of the day and took to her bed early evening. Later, Annie's daughter found her mother 'struggling and kicking as if suffering convulsions.' Neighbours were called to help and another child was sent for Dr Joseph Anderson. Upon examination of Annie, Anderson was of the opinion that she had taken strychnine and went to prepare a remedy for her, but Annie died before he returned.

A life sketch of William Horsford in the dock.

The police were called and during their search of the bed, under the valance, was found a crumpled paper which turned out to be the packet for the poison supplied to Horsford by the chemist. There was also the unsigned note from Horsford, which read: 'Take in a little water: it is quite harmless. Will come over in a day or two.' He denied he was the sender of the 'tonic', but it was proved he was the sender. Brought to the assizes before Justice Hawkins, Horsford was found guilty of murder and sentenced to death.

The execution party entered the condemned cell punctually at 8 o'clock. Horsford walked firmly to the gallows, a warder on each side of him, but no assistance was needed from them. Executioner Billington had completed his duty by the seventh stroke of the hour.

29 JUNE Cures of Fenland Cunning Folk: To Avoid Pregnancy

To avoid an unwanted pregnancy it was suggested the unfortunate girl holds a dead man's hand for two minutes – indeed this was said to be so efficacious the girl would be 'immunised' against fertilisation for two years! Application of vinegar in which pennies from the church collection had been soaked to the woman's most intimate parts was seen as another safeguard.

30 JUNE 1892

William Abbit, a graduate of Downing College, was brought before Cambridge Police Court charged with stealing no less than fifteen books from the reading room of the Cambridge Free Library. He was further charged with stealing thirty-six volumes from the public library of the University of Cambridge. Abbit swore he did not intend to steal them; he just borrowed without a ticket. He was given an excellent character reference by his tutor and an appeal for leniency was requested under the First Offender Act. The Bench sentenced him to four months with hard labour for each case.

JULY

Old Scarlett. In Peterborough Cathedral there is a portrait of long-serving sexton Robert Scarlett, who died 2 July 1591 at the age of 98, 'having buried two generations of his fellow-creatures'.
The Book of Days (1869) states:

Two queens had passed through his hands into that bed which gives a lasting rest to queens and to peasants alike. An officer of Death, who had so long defied his principal, could not but have made some impression on the minds of bishop, dean, prebends, and other magnates of the cathedral.

1 JULY 1737

Mary Bird executed at Ely. Found guilty of murdering her husband John with poison, her crime was subject to punishment under the laws of petty treason. In early modern society every household held its head as the 'Little King' and petty (a corruption of petite) treason (to kill or plot against the head of the household) carried severe penalties; rather than being hanged by the neck until she be dead, she was burnt at the stake. It is a little-known fact that far more women were burnt at the stake for breaching the laws of petty treason than were ever burnt for witchcraft in England.

2 JULY 1644

The Battle of Marston Moor, near York. Many Fen Tigers served in this battle as Cromwell's 'Ironsides', providing the core and backbone of his New Model Army that defeated Prince Rupert's hitherto invincible cavalry; 'as they went down in red ruin against the iron wall of men they had despised as "chawbacons".' Cromwell had claimed to be the champion of the Fens and had argued the cause of the Fenmen, but in fact he was not against the drainage – he was only against the method that was to be used to share the benefits. Fen folk had keenly rallied around Cromwell's banner, but after the war, and despite much blood from the men of the Fens being spilt for him, Cromwell, the Lord Protector, ditched the cause of the Fenmen and an Act was passed in 1649 to enable the Earl of Bedford to undertake the drainage of the Fens.

3 JULY 1817

Findings of the inquest upon the body of William Winter, who had been working in the clunch pit at Melbourn, were published. It transpired that although he had been warned by his master not to work near a particular part of the pit, he had the temerity to go there. A large part of the pit fell in and 'crushed his head to atoms'. A verdict of 'accidental death' was returned.

4 JULY 1786

At about 8.30 p.m., two men from Reach were working in the river about 4 miles from Burwell. They spotted a suspicious man wearing a waterman's jacket; he fled along Reach Lode and disappeared into the fen. The men returned at early light with some neighbours and discovered the body of Elizabeth Hunt (18), a pauper from Burwell workhouse, partially concealed in a hedge, her throat 'cut in a most shocking manner.' The prime suspect was George Miller (18), who had been employed in Brookes's Sedge Gang. Apprehended at Cambridge, he was conducted to the gaol. On the road Miller acknowledged his guilt and soon dictated his confession.

On the night in question, he said, Hunt had come to him and asked, 'would he take her instead of a broomstick?' They walked on, then, at Reach Lode, he threw her in the water, she cried out, and he then dragged her out, cut her throat and put her in the hedge. The coroner's jury returned a verdict of 'wilful murder' against Miller and he was committed to the castle. Curiously, Miller never offered a motive for his crime. It was suggested he had attempted to 'debauch her', but he declared, 'I never made such an attempt nor did it once enter my thoughts.' Brought before the assizes, he was found guilty and executed upon Castle Hill on 4 August, a month to the day after the murder.

5 JULY 1850

An advertisement for a cook wanted for the Royston Union Workhouse, Cambridgeshire, appeared in the local paper:

> She must be a single woman, or widow without encumbrances, of active habits, be able to read and write and be willing to make herself generally useful. Salary £10 per annum. Applications in the party's own handwriting, stating age and previous occupation, accompanied by testimonials as to qualification and character are to be sent to the Clerk of the Union.

6 JULY Punishments of the Past: Transportation

In the early years of the nineteenth century over 200 offences, many of them quite petty misdemeanours such as poaching, sheep stealing or theft, carried the death penalty. As pressure grew to abolish hanging, more and more offences were changed on the statues from the death penalty to transportation. Between 1787 and 1868 thousands of male and female British criminals (some under 10 years of age) were transported in prison hulks to Australia. Locked in irons and laying in dock for months to fill up before departure on the 252 day journey, most were weak and malnourished before the journey even began. As many as a quarter of the passengers would die before they reached Botany Bay.

7 JULY 1892

William Clay (36) was brought before Huntingdon Assizes indicted for the manslaughter of Thomas Parkinson at Woodstone. Both men had been employed at the railway wagon works at Peterborough. They had been drinking at the Cross Keys when they started arguing. Upon leaving pub Clay lashed out at Parkinson, punching him twice and knocking him to the ground. Parkinson was knocked insensible and died the following morning from 'suffusion of blood on the brain', the result, the doctors deposed, of two violent blows on the temples. Clay was found guilty and sentenced to sixteen months' hard labour.

8 JULY 1860

Moses Carter, the Histon Giant, died aged 59. Big and strong, he stood nearly 7ft tall and weighed 23st, but Moses was a gentle giant. He led a simple life tending his land on Histon Moor and earned his living selling the vegetables he grew from a great barrow he wheeled around the area. He was known to carry a coomb (18st) sack of corn under each arm and he pulled his own harrow, saying with pride, 'I don't want no hoss.' Buried in the north-east corner of the churchyard, the great man is still recalled in the local saying: 'Keep quiet here comes Mo Carter, he will cut off your head and put on a cabbage.'

An unfortunate man suffers Peine Fort et Dure.

9 JULY 1741 Punishments of the Past: To Press for an Answer

At the Cambridge Assizes Baron Carter ordered a prisoner, who refused to plead, to have his thumbs twisted with cords. When this failed to extract a plea, the Baron ordered the man be pressed. English courts were in a quandary if suspects refused to plead; if a prisoner pleaded 'guilty' the law stepped in, confiscated their estates and meted out punishment, frequently the death penalty. If they pleaded 'innocence' a trial would ensue, if found guilty the prisoner would be punished and again all possessions were forfeited to the Crown. However, if a defendant remained mute, under the old laws he would stay unconvicted (it was not until 1827 that silence by a defendant was construed as a 'not guilty' plea). This was a powerful incentive for many not to plead and thus *Peine Fort et Dure*, otherwise known as Pressing, became the laws' method of forcing a plea. The victim would be spread and pinioned to the floor of a cell, minimal sustenance given, and over the course of three days weights were piled up upon the chest of the prisoner, leaving him with the agonising choice of plead or die.

10 JULY 1935

The last Cambridge murderer to hang. Walter Osmond Worthington (57) a retired engineer and poultry farmer was executed at Bedford Prison on this day by Thomas Pierrepoint. Tried at Huntingdon Assizes before Mr Justice Hawke on 20 May, Worthington had been found guilty of the murder of his young wife, Sybil Emily Wothington (28), by shooting her at Broughton on 9 March.

Worthington had developed suspicions over her trips to the Crown pub and her relationship with Lionel Wright. On 9 March Sybil had picked up her coat and was going out when Walter challenged her over where she was going and with whom, he had his shotgun in his hand. She did not reply, and moments later a shot was fired. Worthington then took himself to the local rector, confessed what he had done, and the rector took him to St Ives police station where he gave a full statement.

11 JULY John Howard Reports on the Prisons of Cambridgeshire & Huntingdon

Ely Gaol, 1782, gaoler John Allday:

This gaol, the property of the Bishop, who is Lord of the franchise of the Isle of Ely was in part rebuilt by Bishop Mawson in 1768, upon complaint of the cruel method which, for want of a safe gaol, the keeper took to secure his prisoners. This was by chaining them down on their backs upon a floor, across which were several iron bars, with an iron collar with spikes about their necks, and a heavy iron bar over their legs. An excellent magistrate, James Collyer Esq., presented an account of the case, accompanied by a drawing, to the king; with which His Majesty was much affected, and gave immediate orders for a proper enquiry and redress.

For master's-side debtors three rooms up stairs: a room on the same floor for condemned felons. Below stairs is the felons day room; and their cell or night room eighteen and a half feet by ten feet with a window about a foot square. There is a court for felons, with an

The cruel method of securing prisoners at Ely Gaol in the eighteenth century.

offensive sewer. No water-For debtors a court with a pump; but no free ward. No infirmary. No Straw. Clauses against spirituous liquors, and act for preserving the health of prisoners, not hung up. Keeper, a sheriff's officer for the Isle and for the County of Cambridge. No table of fees.

At my last visit, the debtors and felons were together – An unhappy debtor may be an honest man; but, 'Evil communications corrupt good manners.' One of the former was confined for 3s 5½d the charges 8s 3d another, who had a wife and five children, only for costs 4s 9d and gaol fees, 3s 6d.

12 JULY 1833

Inquest held before Mr Twiss upon the body of Samuel Thressold (18). The deceased had suspended a cord with a noose from the rafter of an outbuilding so that, by standing on a beam which extended from one side of the building to the other, he could conveniently place his head in it. This achieved, he tied his own hands behind him and swung himself off. The deceased, 'a well-conducted young man', had never evinced the slightest symptoms of being affected in his intellect; the jury, which was 'a very respectable one' returned a verdict of *felo de se*, and he was accordingly, under the coroner's warrant, buried between the hours of nine and twelve at night and without the observance of religious ceremonies.

13 JULY 1886

William Saunders (29) a coach-body builder was beside himself with grief at the breaking off of his engagement by his fiancée, Alice Pull. Brought to the Huntingdon Assizes in November, the court report stated that Saunders 'was found dogging Miss Pull's footsteps and then rushing upon and stabbing her in a most vital spot near the heart.' He confessed to his crime and made what recompense he could. The judge was impressed and after warning Saunders that, if his stabbing of Miss Pull had proved fatal he would have had no discretion, Justice Field sentenced him to fifteen years.

14 JULY Strange Tales and Folklore of Cambridgeshire: Dog Days

The days from this part of the year (3 July to 11 August) were once known as dog days, when Sirius the 'dog star rages'. In Hone's *Every-Day Book* (1826) a Cambridge contributor to the *Every-Day Book* affirms, that, in the year 1824, an edict was issued there for all persons keeping dogs either to 'muzzle' or 'tie them up', and many a dog was tied up by the neck as a sacrifice; whether to the Mayor or Canicular, this deponent said not; but the act and deed gave rise to the following:

JEU D'ESPRIT
Good mister Mayor
All *dogs* declare
The beam of justice falters!
To miss the *puppies* – sure she's blind,
For *dogs* they are alone consign'd
To *muzzles* or to *halters*!

15 JULY 1817

James Hardy was found guilty at Peterborough Sessions of having in his possession a forged £2 Bank of England note. He was sentenced to seven years transportation.

16 JULY 1832

First major outbreak of Cholera in Wisbech. Jeremiah Jackson wrote:

> The younger Elsum was buried at St Mary's on Sunday night last. His mother, Mrs Hales was attacked on Wednesday morning at 6 o'clock and died the same hour the next morning. At 12 o'clock on Wednesday night Joseph Johnson assisted in giving her a glister and was half suffocated by the stench arising from her body. This morning at 3 o'clock Johnson himself was attacked ... Mrs Hales was buried late on Thursday night at St Mary's being carried from the cart to the grave by J. Christmas, Bliss, Smith and Cox. All four pall-bearers caught the disease. If this is not contagion what is?

It was recorded at the time that forty-one out of 103 cases were fatal. The majority of the victims, including local surgeon Joseph Johnson, were buried in the newly consecrated cemetery in King's Walk.

17 JULY 1926

An inquest was held by the Cambridge Borough Coroner Mr G.A. Wootten at Addenbrooke's Hospital upon the body of the eminent classicist Dr John Percival Postgate, Fellow of Trinity College, Cambridge and editor of *Classical Review* and the *Classical Quarterly*, who had died at the hospital after being knocked down and run over by a steam lorry. The accident had happened opposite Leys School on the Trumpington Road, where the doctor, 'for some unexplained reason', had maintained a diagonal course that took him directly in front of the steam lorry, which was travelling briskly in the same direction. A verdict of 'accidental death' was recorded.

18 JULY 1844

Samuel Baxter (10) was brought before the Huntingdon Assizes and pleaded 'guilty' to an indictment for setting fire to four stacks of straw, the property of Captain Daintree at Hemingford Abbotts. The boys' father was the farm bailiff and there seemed to be no motive for the child's actions. All that was stated in court was a conversation between the boy and the Captain, where young Baxter said he thought the farm house as well as the stacks would be burned 'and then we must go and live in the village.' In passing sentence, Mr Baron Alderson expressed his very great regret in having to do so upon a boy of such tender years but it was 'absolutely necessary that the law should make the same example for boys as it did for men' and sentenced him to fifteen years transportation.

19 JULY 1553

Coronation of Queen Mary I. As Edward VI was dying, Catholic Mary was hunted by Protestant nobleman John Dudley, 1st Duke of Northumberland. She found refuge at Sawston Hall, the home of John Huddleston. Disguising Mary as a dairy maid, he

Queen Mary I – 'Bloody Mary'.

smuggled her out of the hall and away from an angry Protestant mob. As they reached high ground they looked back and saw the hall was a mass of flames and smoke. After her coronation Mary saw to it that that Northumberland was executed and Sawston Hall was rebuilt. Mary restored the Catholic faith to the country and woe betide any remaining Protestants, for they, like the old Sawston Hall, would burn.

20 JULY 1837

John Cole was brought before the assizes for stealing £79 from the house of Mrs Gee, his mistress at Ramsey Fen. Under cover of darkness, Cole had set a ladder against the window of a spare bedroom in which he knew Mrs Gee kept her cash. There was a broken pane and he managed to get his hand through and open the catch. He made good his haul of gold and notes to the value of £79 then covered his tracks, hid the money, and behaved as if nothing had happened. The money was soon found missing, but no suspicion was attached to the servants. That was until about a month later, when Cole said he was going to Chatteris Fair but in fact was caught stepping aboard an American packet steamer with some of the bank notes still in his possession. Found guilty, Cole did get to travel – he was transported for life!

21 JULY 1797

Anna Maria Vassa died on this day aged 4. She was the daughter of Gustavas Vassa (otherwise known as Olaudah Equiano), a man who had been kidnapped from his village in Nigeria at the age of 11 and sold into slavery. Taken to Virginia as a slave he was eventually sold to a ship's captain and travelled widely. After sixteen years as a slave he managed to save enough money to buy his freedom. He came to England and joined the abolitionist cause. His exposé of the infamous slave-ship *Zong*, from which 133 slaves had been thrown overboard in mid-ocean for the insurance money, caused outrage across the nation, but it was to be his a book about his life, *The Interesting Narrative of the Life of Olaudah Equiano* or *Gustavus Vassa the African, written by himself* published in 1789, which became a best-seller and turned many people against slavery and was one of the significant influences upon British lawmakers to abolish the slave trade. Equiano is closely associated with Soham, where he married local girl Susannah Cullen on 7 April 1792.

Olaudah Equiano.

22 JULY 1801

In the late 1790s a series of daring and skilful robberies, from apparently locked and secure rooms, which accrued some considerable hauls, were carried out in a number of the Cambridge colleges. It was only with increased public vigilance, following two handsome rewards of 100 guineas and 500 guineas put up by the university, that residents of Bell Lane reported their suspicions of Richard Kidman. Once in custody he gave up his accomplices, chimneysweep William Grimshaw and pedlar Henry Cohen, who sold the plunder. Thus the team and their methods revealed Grimshaw entered the locked rooms by climbing down the chimneys. Kidman was skilled with his hands in the picking of locks. Cohen was the assistant and 'carry man'.

Grimshaw was tried first: found guilty, he was sentenced to death. Kidman was also found guilty and received the capital sentence, commuted to imprisonment on account of his early co-operation. No charge would stick to Cohen and he walked free.

23 JULY 1863

A broadsheet was published relating to the recent case of Alfred Gunn, who was brought before the Assize Court, Cambridge, on indictments of unlawfully wounding PCs Ebenezer Danby, William Vialls and George Williams with intent to do them grievous bodily harm on 21 March 1863. PC Danby had brought Gunn into custody after a drunken altercation in a brothel. Gunn's mother found out where her son was and rushed to the police station, where, soon after her arrival, she appeared to go into a fit. Gunn was 're-excited' and immediately pulled a razor out of his pocket and gashed all three of the constables, catching them about their mouths and cheeks. It appeared that the prisoner was almost stone deaf; and it was very doubtful he heard the policemen order him to leave the brothel and the jury considered his outburst at the station house was caused by the sight of his mother's condition. The jury acquitted Gunn of the more serious charge, but found him 'guilty of wounding without intent.'

24 JULY 1849

George Shaw, described as 'a man of unusual stature and strength', was arraigned at the Crown Court charged with murdering Ann Simms by knocking her down and kicking and trampling upon her on 6 July at Melbourn. Joel King testified:

> I was at Melbourne Feast. I was coming down the village at one in the morning with Ellis Bysoath. I saw the prisoner and a woman with him. Near Mr Wood's house I saw the prisoner knock the woman down ... He kicked her several times, and said, 'I will kick your damn guts out.' He kicked her with all his force. After this he said to her 'Get up will you.' After a short exchange he dragged the woman up, she appeared very weak then ... When we got within 100 yards of the Bull's Head Inn we heard a noise. We heard a man's voice swearing and then we heard a woman scream out, 'Pray George, do not kill me, perhaps I may do better next time.'

Joseph Prior, landlord of the Bull, stated:

> I saw a man hunting a woman round the horse trough. It was the prisoner. The trough is six yards from the house and stands a yard from some palisades, so he could just catch her across it. He kept striking her, till he knocked her down. She kept crying out 'Don't George,

don't hit me' and crept under the horse trough. The poor thing crept under it like a dog ... I opened the window and said to him 'You leering hound you – do you mean killing the woman?'

In reply, Shaw had clawed up a few stones as if ready to hurl them up and threatened to smash out Prior's brains if he said another word. Shaw then dragged the woman out from under the trough and set off up the road kicking and cursing her. Maria Howe called the doctor and nursed Ann until she died a few days later. John Deighton, the town surgeon, attested to the wounds and bruising that belied the beating Ann had suffered.

The post-mortem revealed that she died of 'an effusion of blood on the brain.' After a long speech for the defence and summing up from the judge, the jury retired and returned a verdict of 'guilty of manslaughter'. Shaw burst into tears. Even the judge seemed surprised at the verdict and, with steely eyes, congratulated Shaw on evading the capital charge. But then he addressed the prisoner in the most solemn tones, reminding Shaw that morally he had committed 'the most atrocious offence toward the victim of his violence' and that 'under these circumstances it was the duty of the Court to remove him forever from the country which he had polluted with his crimes.' Shaw was transported to a penal colony for the rest of his life.

25 JULY 1741

John Goddes was executed upon the gallows at Mill Common, Huntingdon, for highway robbery. Ninety years to the day, in 1832, John Nunn, Simeon Nunn and Ephraim Litchfield were capitally indicted at Cambridge Assizes for assaulting Henry Thurnall on the highway between Whittlesford to Royston and stealing his watch and various monies. At the assize the three men really had no case for their defence. All were found guilty. John Nunn and Ephraim Litchfield were sentenced to death, Simeon Nunn was eighteen and he was saved from the gallows on account of his age and was sentenced to transportation for life.

26 JULY 1833

Name withheld. The charge against 'a lady' for purloining two teaspoons belonging to the corporation of Huntingdon at a ball given to celebrate Lord Sandwich attaining his majority was brought before the assizes, but she was not named in the press. The prisoner was one of the persons invited to the ball and, the case being proved against her, she was convicted and sentenced to ten weeks' imprisonment.

27 JULY 1790

Eleanor Godwin, found guilty of assaulting and robbing Thomas Hitchcock of 25 guineas and some silver while upon the highway at Spaldwicke, was capitally convicted and left for execution. Henry Dixon was ordered to be transported for seven years after being found guilty of robbing the stable of Henry Dixon. John Gee was ordered to the House of Correction for six months for stealing six geese. Richard Carr was imprisoned for twelve months for passing counterfeit money. Robert Thompson and Mary Griffin got six months each for a similar offence and John and Robert Jones, confined on suspicion of sheep stealing, were permitted to enlist as soldiers.

A chap-book illustration of witches and their cat familiars.

28 JULY 1659

The Longstanton Witch Trial. Margaret Pryor of Longstanton had spread the story of how Widow Morlin, a Quaker, had taken her from her bed one night, put a bridle into her mouth and changed her into a bay mare and, with other Quakers, had ridden her the 4 miles to Maddingley Hall. Fastening her to a latch on the door, the Quakers then went inside and feasted on mutton, rabbits and lamb. Egged on by other locals who were opposed to the Quakers, the matter was brought before the assizes and Pryor repeated her story to Justice Wyndham. No doubt intrigued, Wyndham humoured Pryor and enquired the details of her experience, such as if she had become dirty when ridden upon or perhaps her hands or feet made sore. Pryor solemnly replied that her feet had been made sore but not her hands and that she had remained clean.

Wyndham then asked why Pryor had not been further used in such a way since, to which she replied she had burnt some elder bark with some of her own hair and thus by this magic process prevented Widow Morlin having further power over her. The judge had heard enough and challenged her that, by her own confession of using magic, Pryor was revealing *herself* as a sorcerer! In his summary Justice Wyndham described Pryor as 'a whimsical woman' and concluded the whole affair 'a mere dream and a fantasy.' The jury were not convinced either and the Quakers were found not guilty and acquitted.

29 JULY 1864

William Morley Wallis was indicted for the murder of Maria Hunt and assault with intent to murder on Sally Harris Walker. The charges dated back to 28 February when two elderly ladies, Mrs Hunt (78) and Mrs Walker (70), who lived together in Prospect

Cottage between Prospect Row and Melbourn Place on the north side of Parker's Piece, were attacked in the evening by a man wearing a mask. Their sixteen-year-old servant girl went for help and brought neighbours running. Both ladies had been severely beaten. Inside the house a man's hat, an oilcloth mask, a knife and an undertaker's cloak were discovered, but no culprit. In the morning light footprints and a bludgeon were found outside.

William Morley Wallis became a suspect because he was seen in the area on the night in question, and when his home was searched more oilcloth of the type found at the scene and a crape mask with eye holes was discovered. Wallis was arrested and awaited his fate. Mrs Hunt had died of her injuries, but had given a statement before she succumbed to her wounds. Mrs Walker survived and was assisted into court, but could not positively say that Wallis was their attacker. The judge was scrupulously careful in his summing up, it really was down to the jury and they decided the evidence against Wallis was just too circumstantial and that there was no witness or firm proof that he was the man in the house and they returned a verdict of 'not guilty' and Wallis was acquitted. No murderer nor any motive for this attack on two old ladies was ever identified.

30 JULY 1910

Appeals are launched for the whereabouts of Walter Eli Bedder (50) of Newbury, Berkshire, who had been missing since 25 July. His body was eventually found in a lane by Milton Woods in early August. His identity was established from a number stamped upon a keyring registered with a London insurance office found in his pocket. The post-mortem indicated death was primarily caused by an irritant poison and secondly heart disease. A verdict in accordance with the medical evidence was returned.

31 JULY 1884

A shoemaker named Matthews was brought before the Cambridge Assizes indicted for wounding his wife with intent to kill her. On 6 May Matthew's wife had been in a distressed state for most of the day; this was not an uncommon event as she had attempted to commit suicide once before. During the night she entered a bedroom in which her nephew was sleeping, she was bleeding from the neck, screaming and crying out 'my husband has cut my throat and his own too!' A bloody razor was found in the bedroom she shared with her husband. The old man was found with his neck cut too. Both were removed to hospital where, unable to speak, it was claimed he wrote on a slate 'I meant to do for her, but was stopped.' Both recovered from their wounds, but at the trial the hysterical and confused testimony of the wife was ordered to be dismissed by the judge and a serious question was raised over the authenticity of the message claimed to have been written by Matthews. However, the medical evidence was against Matthews, the surgeon was of the opinion that Mrs Matthews could not have inflicted the wounds she displayed upon herself. The jury found Matthews guilty and the judge sentenced him to fifteen years' penal servitude. His wife was carried out of court crying and shrieking loudly.

AUGUST

The Eynesbury Giant, James Toller, was born on Rectory Lane, Eynesbury on 28 August 1795. Born to parents of average height, by the age of ten James stood over 5ft tall. James kept on growing; by the time he was eighteen he stood over 8ft tall, each of his feet measured 15in in length. At the age of twenty he stood a massive 8ft 10in (although it has been suggested the most reliable recorded height he achieved was 8ft 6in). He was put on public exhibition as 'The Young English Giant' in London in the autumn of 1815 and was presented to the Emperor of Russia and the King of Prussia. Sadly he died young on 4 February 1819 and is buried under the centre of the nave in Eynesbury Parish Church.

1 AUGUST 1741

Isaac West was executed on Castle Hill, Cambridge, for the murder of his wife.

2 AUGUST 1786

The body of Jervaise Matcham was hanged in chains from the gibbet at Alconbury. In 1780 Matcham was a private soldier in the 49th Regiment and had been sent on escort duty with Benjamin Jones, the drummer boy, to collect money for supplies from Major Reynolds at Diddington Hall. Entrusted with £7 in gold coins, Matcham led the drummer boy to some secluded land between Alconbury and Brampton, cut his throat, and made off with the gold. Matcham made good his escape and joined the Navy.

Years later, Matcham had been paid off and was travelling with a companion across Salisbury Plain at night. At to a crossroads the ghost of the drummer boy appeared. Terrified, Matcham fled to the nearest pub and confessed to the people inside. Arrested and returned to Huntingdon for trial as a deserter of the 49th, he was made to wear their scarlet jacket for the proceedings.

Found guilty of the murder, Matcham was hanged and then placed in a gibbet cage on the site of the murder, still wearing the military uniform. The gibbet used in this particular instance was an unusual one for it consisted of a sturdy beam of wood

The ghost of the drummer boy murdered by Jervaise Matcham confronts his killer on Salisbury Plain.

*Jervaise Matcham in his gibbet cage
near Alconbury in the late 1780s.*

secured between the branches of two elm trees. A swivel in the centre of the fixing chain to the cage above Matcham's head allowed the cage to swing and twist in the wind. An eyewitness to this sight recorded:

> It often used to frit me as a land and I have seen horses frit with it. The coach and carriage people were always on the look-out for it, but it was never my taste. Oh yes! I can mind it rotting away, bit by bit, and the red rags flapping from it. After a while they took it down and very pleased I were to see the last of it.

3 AUGUST 1837

The Times reported that Conservatives were persecuted at Cambridge:

> The Whig-Radical party are not content with the victory they have obtained, but are pursuing a system of most vexatious prosecution against those who opposed them. The magistrates are almost daily occupied in investigating charges arising out of the election, and as it so happens that the mayor and most of the acting magistrates are strong Whigites, the chances are somewhat against the Conservatives obtaining a calm and impartial decision.

4 AUGUST 1895

At Wansford near Peterborough three cyclists, namely Fred Bowman, John Scholey and L.S. Smith, respectively from Huddersfield, Bradford and Leeds, were riding a triple-cycle to London. While descending a hill into Wansford along the Great North Road they encountered a number of men assembled for an Oddfellows festival. The cyclists rang their bell but one man, a Stamford publican, George Hodge, hesitated and stepped in front of them. He was knocked down and was so seriously injured he died the following morning.

5 AUGUST 1895

Miss Adelaide 'Addie' Bassett (36), a London parachutist, was killed at a fête held at Peterborough. The display, which consisted of a balloon ascent and a double parachute descent, was billed as 'A Race For Life' and was to be performed by Captain Alfred Orton and Miss Bassett. As the balloon ascended it was noticed that a telephone wire caught on Miss Bassett's parachute, causing it to turn upside down. At a height of 60ft they jumped. Captain Orton's parachute allowed him to glide to the earth, but because they were jumping from such a low height the crucial seconds lost by the inversion of her parachute meant Miss Bassett's did not inflate correctly and she fell head first, hitting the ground with a sickening thud. Removed to an infirmary, she was found to be dead.

This terrible scene was witnessed by thousands of spectators. Both Orton and Bassett were experienced parachutists; Miss Bassett had made over thirty successful descents. The inquest jury returned a verdict of 'accidental death' adding 'since no useful purpose is served by these senseless exhibitions, at which the lives of performers are risked, they should be made illegal.'

6 AUGUST 1819

Execution of Thomas Weems for the murder of his wife Mary Ann – or no rest for the wicked. Hanged shortly after twelve noon over the gateway of the country gaol before a vast crowd, Weems was left to swing for the statutory hour then was cut down and immediately conveyed in a cart, under escort from the sheriff's officers and constables, to the Chemical Lecture Room in the Botanical Garden. Professor Cumming had prepared a powerful galvanic battery and before an invited and learned audience performed a number of experiments, whereby an electric current was passed through various parts of the executed man's body. The results were keenly observed.

When galvanic stimulus was applied to the supraorbitary nerve (beneath the eyebrow), and the heel, the most extraordinary grimaces were exhibited every time that the electric discharges were made; 'every muscle in his face was simultaneously thrown into fearful action: rage, horror, despair, anguish, and ghastly smiles united their hideous expressions in the murderer's face, surpassing the wildest representations of the Fuseli or a Kean.'

The following day the body was opened and placed on public view, no pity for the killer was recorded from the crowds who passed through, just their feelings of 'curiosity, disgust and awe.' The doors were then shut and a large group of learned gentlemen observed Mr Okes perform an extensive dissection of the body (*see also* 17 May).

7 AUGUST 1775

John Stickwood was convicted of the murder of Andrew Nunn and the death sentence passed upon him. He was executed four days later upon Castle Hill, Cambridge.

Captain Orton gazes down upon the prostrate body of fellow parachutist Miss Adelaide Bassett after her parachute failed.

8 AUGUST 1812

Execution of Daniel Dawson at Cambridge Castle. Dawson was a tout who lodged on Newmarket High Street. Persuaded by a villainous bookie named Bland to prevent some heavily backed horses owned Richard Prince from running, he enlisted the help of 'a ramshackle old chemist named Bishop.' Learning how to dissolve arsenic in water, he mixed some of the poison in Prince's horse trough.

After Prince received some intimation of the poisoning attempt he did not permit use of the trough, but by the following day Prince decided the poisoning attempt was 'all gammon' and decided to let the horses drink from the trough. In the meantime, Dawson thought the arsenic was too weak and had visited again to 'hot up' the potency of the poison by adding more! Some of the horses knew something was amiss and would not drink; some drank a little and were seized by violent griping. The horses of Sir Sitwell Sitwell were dosed with castor oil and recovered, but tragically the orders for Sir Frank Standish's horses to wait for Dr Bowles of Cambridge proved fatal and the horses died in agony.

The Jockey Club offered a 500 guinea reward for information. Evidence was soon accumulated against Dawson and he was sent to Cambridge Assizes on four indictments for poisoning a horse belonging to Mr Adams, of Royston, Herts, and a

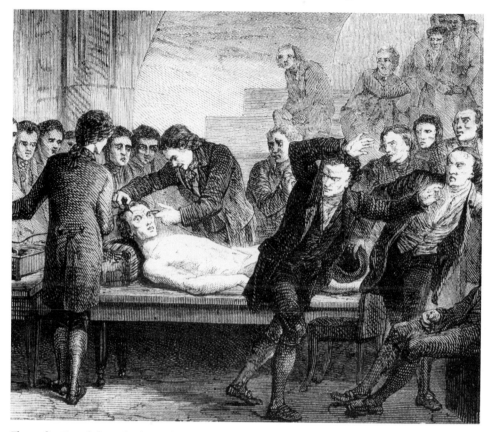

The application of electrodes for a galvanic experiment upon a corpse.

blood mare belonging to Mr Northey, at Newmarket, in 1809; and also for poisoning a horse belonging to Sir Frank Standish, and another belonging to Lord Foley in 1811, at the same place. Dawson always swore he did not intend to kill the horses, but simply to slow them down or make them temporarily ill.

Tried on the first case only, Bishop turned King's Evidence and sealed Dawson's fate. Before execution Dawson admitted poisoning horses at Doncaster a couple of years previously. A scaffold was specially erected on top of Cambridge Castle and Dawson was hanged before a crowd of some 15,000 spectators.

9 AUGUST 1853

Police investigations continue to ascertain the identity of the body of a young woman found a few days earlier in a field on Portley Hill near Littleport. At the inquest Dr Cadazo revealed his findings from the post-mortem examination. The wounds upon the side of her head had not been fatal; death had been caused by her swallowing 6½oz of Prussic Acid. In September it was reported that the police had still not ascertained the identity of the woman, the reconvened inquest jury returned a verdict 'that the deceased woman, unknown to the jurors, came to her death by blows and poison feloniously administered to her by some person and persons unknown.'

Daniel Dawson at the time of his trial.

10 AUGUST 1745

Henry Footmass and John Jerroms were executed before a large crowd upon Castle Hill for highway robbery.

11 AUGUST 1792

Edward Course was executed upon Castle Hill for the rape of Sarah Ellis. On this same day in 1849 the *Cambridge Chronicle* contained this carefully worded news item from Elsworth:

> This little village has for the last two or three weeks been kept in a bustle of excitement, owing to a rumour that the not very reverend shepherd of a dissenting flock had fallen from his high estate, and had yielded to the delusions and temptations of the evil one. The possession was evinced by the reverend gentleman making an indecent assault upon the person of a young girl 16 years of age, who resided with him as domestic servant. The girl with great prudence and determination frustrated his design, and proceeding to the house of her parents, immediately acquainted them with what had occurred. The reverend gentleman was taxed with the offence, and he made the most abject solicitations that the matter should not be exposed, and promised amendment. The girl returned to

his roof, but shortly afterwards the offence was repeated. The poor girl as before left his roof and returned to that of her now irate parents, who published the transaction far and wide. As may be easily imagined, a general feeling of execration was engendered, and the offender has resigned his charge to save himself from being expelled.

12 AUGUST 1775

Reported case of Thomas Newman brought before the court for breaking into the dwelling-house of Mr Harper, shoemaker, at Melbourn, in the dead of night, and stealing two pairs of men's and one pair of women's shoes. Found guilty and sentenced to death, he was reprieved and ordered for transportation for fourteen years.

13 AUGUST John Howard Reports on the Prisons of Cambridgeshire & Huntingdon

Ely Bridewell, last visited in 1782 (built 1651) consists of one room below for men (16 feet by 15 feet 4 inches); and two above for women. No water accessible to prisoners; prison out or repair. No court; one might be made for the keeper's large garden. In February 1776, a women sick: no apothecary. No allowance. Clauses of act against spirituous liquors not hung up. Keeper's salary £10: no fees.

14 AUGUST 1895

An inquest was held at the Red Lion in Grantchester, with Coroner Algernon J. Lyon presiding. Francis Iltid Nicholl (32) an undergraduate of Clare College, had met his death by drowning in the Granta. Nicholl and been boating at Byron's Pool with fellow undergraduate Thomas Knight. Nicholl volunteered to skull back. After going two or three strokes he caught a bad 'crab' that caused him to fall backwards and upset the boat. Knight swam a few strokes, but turning to see where his friend was saw him flailing his arms in the water. Knight went back and grabbed his friend's collar, but the water was deeper than he expected and they both sank. Nicholl clutched hold of Knight, but he got free and managed to get hold of a stake and pulled himself onto the bank in a fainting condition. He saw nothing more of Nicholl. The jury returned a verdict of 'accidentally drowned'.

15 AUGUST 1874

Fortean Cambridgeshire. Among the archives of Charles Fort, the great collector of all things strange and anomalous, is preserved a report from the *Scientific American* that states that ants (some of them wingless) fell like rain upon Cambridge in the summer of 1874.

16 AUGUST 1853 Report of the Prison Inspectors

Ely House of Correction, 1853:

Number of Prisoners at time of Inspection: 13 Males and 1 Female.
There have been no alterations in the buildings or in the discipline of the prison since the last inspection. The window at the west end of the corridor, through which the two prisoners effected their escape in November 1852, had not been made secure at the time

Raining cats, dogs and pitchforks ... but not ants.

of my visit, but the Governor assured me that it had been determined to fix some iron bars outside immediately to effect that object.

The Governor appointed to succeed Mr Lipscomb was formerly a superintendent of the county police; he appears to be well qualified for the office.

The wards, cells and all parts of the prison were clean and in good order; the provisions were of good quality; the daily cost of the food was 3¼d per head.

The general health of the prisoners has been good; there was one male prisoner under medical treatment at the time of my visit to the prison.

There has been no change in the duties performed by the chaplain. He expresses himself well satisfied with the turnkeys, who continue to instruct the prisoners in their cells. The chief turnkey instructs the more advanced prisoners, while the under turnkey attend to those who are just learning to read and write. They receive £7 10s per annum each for this additional duty.

The general conduct of the prisoners is represented to be orderly and submissive; they made no complaints. The number of punishments for prison offences was 26. Mat making has been extended and some prisoners are mending the prison clothes but they are not all kept fully employed and having no light in their cells they continue to pass too much time in bed during the winter.

17 AUGUST 1855

Burwell's PC, Richard Peak, was ordered by his sergeant to attend an auction of crops at the Lion pub in Wicken. He left Burwell in his uniform but, according to witnesses, he attended the auction in his civilian clothes, the police in his particular force were given license to wear their 'private clothes' when on night duty in order to save their day uniforms. At 3.15 a.m. Peak finally bade farewell to the landlord of the Lion, saying 'Good morning; I've got an hour and a half's walk, and then I will go to bed.' He left and was never seen again.

He had been due to report in to his sergeant at Burwell at 4 a.m., but when he failed to do so a search was instigated, but nothing was found. Some men were said to have been seen fighting at Wicken around 4 a.m., but could not say if Peak was one of them. PC Peak left a pregnant wife and one child. The following year a local man called for an officer to attend his death bed, he said he knew who killed PC Peak, and that he had been hit on the head and burnt to ashes in the brick kiln at Burwell Fen.

Another tale suggests the unfortunate constable was killed and wheeled in a barrow to a deep pond or fen ditch, where his body was weighted down and tipped into the murky depths. A human skeleton with severe damage to the skull was reportedly found in a pond at Wicken in the 1880s. The skeleton was quietly returned to its watery grave without any officials being informed. Another skeleton, potentially that of the missing constable, was found during excavations at the Anchor pub on the Wicken side of Burwell; the skull was displayed over the bar, but was dropped and smashed. What happened to the other bones is not known.

PC Richard Peak, the lost constable of Burwell.

18 AUGUST 1800

James Thompson escaped from Ely Gaol at about 1 a.m. The wanted poster detailed he was:

> ... aged about 30 years, about 5 feet and a half high, rather thin, long visage, of a fair and ruddy complexion, black eyes and coal black hair, has a scar hardly visible on the right eye brow, and another scar on the left side of the mouth downwards; and had on at the time he escaped, a snuff coloured coat, a yellow ground striped waistcoat, corduroy breeches, a pair of new shoes and a very good round hat.

The notice concluded:

> Whoever will apprehend the said James Thompson, shall receive a reward of ten guineas, to be paid on his being safely lodged in any of his Majesty's Goals [sic] by John Leaford, Keeper of the Goal at Ely.

19 AUGUST 1915

Blind Motorist. Mr Alfred Keeble, farmer and coal merchant of Duxford, was summonsed to Cambridge Police Court for driving a motorcar without a license. It turned out that he could not obtain one on account that he had been blind since the previous January. When he had been caught the car was being steered by a fully sighted girl of 11 years. Mr Keeble said the car was quite easy to drive – as long as someone told him which way to steer or steer for him. The magistrates fined him 40s. Keeble said he would prefer to go to prison rather than pay the fine – the request was refused.

20 AUGUST 1880

Elizabeth Knowles was brought before Cambridge Assizes charged with the wilful murder of a female child at March on 20 August 1879. Knowles was a domestic servant, she was married, but her husband, a native of America, had returned to the States upon the understanding that she would follow him some time later. She carried on in service, but when signs of pregnancy began to show she denied it was anything of the sort.

On 24 October the body of a child was discovered in a dyke in Hurst Lane, about 2 miles from March railway station. There was a bruise over the child's eye and its nose was flattened. In his examination, Dr Easby concluded the child had either been suffocated before she was put in the dyke or was drowned. Suspicions were raised against Knowles, the American police were contacted and on March 15 1880 Elizabeth Knowles voluntarily returned to England. She gave a statement that the child had been seized by a convulsive fit while on the train between Whittlesea and March. At March she found the child appeared to have died. After some hours she was sure this was the case and, wishing to keep the birth from her husband, threw the body of the baby into the dyke where it was discovered. At her trial, Dr Easby could not positively affirm the child did not die in the manner suggested by the prisoner. Baron Pollock, in an exhaustive charge, detailed the facts and the grand jury, after a long deliberation, ignored the bill and Elizabeth Knowles was discharged.

21 AUGUST 1821

Fourteen members of a notorious gang that had terrorised the neighbourhood of Soham for the past two years were apprehended upon information given by an informant. By the time the case came to trial twenty-two men were in custody charged with stealing fowls, sacks of malt, turkeys, a wooden measure, tools and various articles belonging to householders in Snailwell, Exning, Freckenham, Fordham, Wicken and Soham. Sixteen were found guilty. William Day was sentenced to death for the burglary of William Delphs at Wicken; this was, however, commuted to transportation along with Thomas Isaacson and his sons George and Edward, and Sam Wright the elder and Sam Wright the younger, Henry and John Attlesey, James Bailey, William West, William Arnold, William Worlledge and John Thurston. Richard Cater was sentenced to ten months' imprisonment with hard labour while William Webb and William Canham each received seven months.

22 AUGUST Punishments of the Past: Fines for Profanity

Much was made of the laws against profanities in the eighteenth and nineteenth centuries. The fee table used by the Cambridgeshire Magistrates under the Profane Oaths Act of 1745 notes the following scale of fines:

For a first offence –
By a day labourer, common soldier, sailor or seaman   1/-
By a person under the degree of Gentleman   2/-
Every person of or above the degree of Gentleman   5/-
For a second offence the fines were doubled and a third trebled.

23 AUGUST 1935 Grim Tales of Cambridgeshire: Spinney Abbey

During the summer of 1935 the north wing of Spinney Abbey showed signs of subsidence and it was decided to under-pin the north wall. While digging out the foundations a number of skeletons were uncovered. One who was there recorded:

On digging out the first hole we found 3 skeletons close together; directly under the house wall was the remains of a powerful man of about 19 years of age, close to this the skeletons of a smaller man and on the outside the remains of a child about 9 or 10 years, all in a space of about 3 feet long and 2 feet wide. Their feet and legs were near the skulls and all face downwards. We arrived at the probable age of the skeleton under the wall as 19 years by the fact his wisdom teeth were just coming through. The skull of this man was broken in at the side and cracked across. We concluded this happened before burial.

24 AUGUST 1930

Reports published of the inquest held into the death of George Rolfe (38), a fishmonger of St Matthew's Street, Cambridge who died in Addenbrooke's Hospital after eating what he thought were edible mushrooms. The coroner called upon Emmanuel College botany lecturer Mr F.T. Brooks to give his opinion. Mr Brooks stated it was difficult to explain the difference between edible and inedible fungi; unfortunately the mushrooms consumed by Mr Rolfe were 'most dangerous to eat ... some of the most poisonous in existence.' Dr McNeill gave the cause of death as gastro enteritis and atrophy of the liver, which was 'absolutely destroyed.' The coroner recorded 'Death by misadventure.'

25 AUGUST Grim Tales of Cambridgeshire: Ned Bonnet

Ned Bonnet was born into a reputable family in the Isle of Ely. He was educated and had been set up as a grocer in the county. Ruined by a fire and not being in a condition to retrieve his loss, he went to London to avoid creditors and fell in with a gang of highwaymen. After a chance meeting with a young baker's son named Zachary Clare, Bonnet could see the boy sought adventure, took him under his wing and together they enacted some 300 robberies around Cambridgeshire. They had great success working together for three or four years and became 'such a terror to the people of the Isle of Ely that they durst hardly stir out far from home, unless they were half a dozen or half a score in a body together.'

Clare was captured while undertaking a robbery alone, but gave up Ned Bonnet to save his own neck. Caught at his London lodgings on Old Street, Bonnet was committed to Newgate then conveyed to Cambridge for trial before Mr Baron Lovet. Found guilty he was executed at the castle on 28 March 1713, 'to the general joy and satisfaction of all the people in that county.' Clare's near-brush with the gallows did not set him onto a law-abiding course and soon he was back robbing coaches around London. When it became 'too hot' for him, he worked in Wales and finally moved to Warwickshire,

Stand and deliver!

where he was wounded by a blast from Sir Humphrey Jennison's coachman during an attack on his coach. Taken to gaol, tried and found guilty of highway robbery, Clare ended his days on the Warwick gallows in 1715.

26 AUGUST 1839

An inquest was held at Ely upon the body of Martha Day, a girl of about 13. At about 1 p.m. the previous day she had called out to her mother. Rushing outside, her mother found her standing on a low branch of an apple tree in the orchard. On lifting her down from the tree the girl could not stand and appeared to have lost the use of her limbs; before she could be carried into the house she expired. The post-mortem made by Messrs Muriel revealed a dislocation at the first vertebra of the neck had occurred, causing total paralysis and almost instant death, the verdict was given accordingly.

27 AUGUST 1790

The findings of the Summer Assizes at Huntingdon were published in *The Times*:

> Eleanor Godmin, for assaulting Thomas Hitchcock on the highway in the parish of Spaldwicke, and robbing him of 25 guineas and some silver was capitally convicted, and left for execution; Henry Dixon, for robbing the stable of Henry Speed was ordered to be transported for seven years; John Gee for stealing six geese was ordered to the House of Correction for six months; Richard Carr, for putting off counterfeit money, to be imprisoned 12 months, and find sureties for his good behaviour for 12 months more; Robert Thompson and Mary Griffin for a similar offence, to be imprisoned for six months and find sureties for 12 months more; John and Robert Jones confined on suspicion of sheep stealing were permitted to enlist as soldiers; and six prisoners were discharged.

28 AUGUST 1873

William Ison (29) was struck by lightning and killed while cutting hay upon Quy Fen. A more timely departure after a long life was that of Henry Sidgwick, English Utilitarian philosopher on this day in 1900. Sidgwick studied with distinction at Trinity College, where he became a member of the Cambridge Apostles. Elected to a fellowship at Trinity, he was a lecturer in classics there for ten years. A member of the Metaphysical Society, he was one of the founders and first president of the Society for Psychical Research. Founded in 1882, the purpose of the society was to encourage scientific research into psychic or paranormal phenomena in order to establish their truth and history. Research was initially aimed at six areas: telepathy, mesmerism and similar phenomena, mediums, apparitions, physical phenomena associated with séances and the history of such phenomena.

29 AUGUST 1636

The Great Fire of Little Whyte. 'Fifteen commoning tenements' were burnt down and others damaged.

30 AUGUST 1746

William Budge was executed upon the gallows at Mill Common, Huntingdon for the murder of his wife, Ann.

31 AUGUST Strange Tales and Folklore of Cambridgeshire: Ball Lightening

Stories of strange burning balls of fire have been handed down through generations of Fen folk. One incident related to me was from a lady who, as a young girl in the 1930s, was living on a farm on the Cambridgeshire and Norfolk borders near Southery.

The memorial stone for
William Ison on Quy Fen.

One harvest time there was a flash of lightening and a fiery sphere, about the size of a cricket ball, came out of nowhere and headed straight for the barn. Workmen and the girl watched transfixed as the fiery ball seemed to fly around 'as if bouncing off the walls' then flew out again and disappeared. The phenomena occurred over a matter of seconds. They rushed to the barn and all present were amazed, not just at what they had seen, but also because the intense ball of fire they had witnessed had not set the whole barn ablaze. There was evidence of where the strange fiery ball had touched with small scorch marks or charred hay, but nothing more. The physical nature or even the existence of ball lightening remains a contentious subject among scientists; some of whom consider the phenomenon to be caused by atmospheric electrical conditions.

SEPTEMBER

Cambridge Prison staff, c. 1910.

1 SEPTEMBER 1827

Joshua Slade (18) is executed upon the Huntingdon Gallows for the murder of his master, the Revd Joshua Waterhouse (81), at Little Stukeley. Slade had been a servant to Waterhouse since he was 15. Waterhouse was a miser and to many a bad payer. Slade planned to rob his employer. He obtained a sword and hid himself in a room within the house to wait for the old man to go to bed. Unfortunately Slade fell asleep and the old man heard his snoring and entered the room with a blunderbuss. Slade held out his sword to the old man stating, 'if you will forgive me I will forgive you, but if not, this is your death warrant.' Waterhouse replied, 'I will suffer anything first' and with that sealed his fate – Slade ran him through then stabbed him repeatedly.

Believing Waterhouse to be dead Slade carried his body to a large brewing vat in the cellar, threw it in and fled. The body of the reverend was discovered the following morning, he had not died immediately and had attempted to get out of the vat, but he had succumbed in the attempt and was found half in and half out.

When questioned, Slade said he was visiting his sister in Godmanchester, but she could not confirm his alibi. Charged with the murder of Revd Waterhouse, Slade appeared before the Assize, but pleaded his innocence. He was found guilty, but there were lingering legal doubts over how robust the conviction was, based on the evidence presented at the trial. His execution was twice delayed, but the prison chaplain breached confidence and leaked Slade's condemned-cell confession to the authorities and Slade went to the gallows. His body was handed to the anatomists, his skin was flayed from his corpse, tanned and sold as grim souvenirs and his skeleton displayed in a travelling show.

Joshua Slade.

Part of the execution rope and a strip of tanned skin from Joshua Slade.

2 SEPTEMBER 1910

Rung out. The death is announced of Abraham Howard (86), the resident bell ringer of St Peter's, Wisbech for the last twenty years. He rang all the chimes from the workmen's bell at 5.45 a.m. to the curfew at 8.45 p.m. He would ascend and descend the thirty-six steps to the belfry four to six times a day; his work necessitated 2,000 visits to the belfry annually. He had retired from ringing for two years previously and was also a cobbler by trade. He had a family of eighteen children.

3 SEPTEMBER 1887

Harvest Tragedy. Reports were published of the death of a lad named William Rogers of Littleport, who was killed after accidentally falling into the blades of a reaping machine.

4 SEPTEMBER Tales from the Gaols

Under the Youthful Offenders Act (1854) offenders under 16 could be sent to Reformatory Schools for between two and five years, after fourteen days in prison. The Reformatory Schools were administered by voluntary bodies with aid from state grants. Punishment was an essential part of the strict regime, which included freezing cold baths, military style drills and hard physical labour. In 1861 a further Act was passed and different categories of children were included:

Any child apparently under the age of fourteen found begging or receiving alms.

Any child apparently under the age of fourteen found wandering and not having any home or visible means of support, or in company of reputed thieves.

Any child apparently under the age of twelve whom, having committed an offence punishable by imprisonment or less.

Any child under the age of fourteen whose parents declare him to be beyond their control.

In 1866 the Industrial School Act created establishments for orphans, children of convicted criminals and refractory children who would be subject to a strictly instructed basic education and training in industrial and agricultural processes. By the 1870s there were fifty industrial schools for 2,500 needy children and sixty-five Reformatory Schools detaining about 5,000 young offenders. Despite these best efforts, juveniles were still being sent to prison well into the 1890s. The Borstal system of reformatory prisons for young offenders guilty of serious or repeat offences was introduced in 1900.

5 SEPTEMBER 1832

Sergeant Major Briggs, 1st Dragoon Guards, shot himself through the heart with his horse pistol when en route from Peterborough to Spalding while the troop had stopped. At the inquest it was deposed that the deceased had appeared mentally disturbed and had expressed 'some uneasiness' about his ability to perform the duties of his rank; he had only been promoted for three days. The jury returned a verdict that 'he destroyed himself in a fit of lunacy.'

6 SEPTEMBER 1829

Harvest Festival celebrations at Warboys took a nasty turn. William Angel (23) attempted to quell the disturbance, but was met with punches and kicks. A mob of about fifty people ended up in front of Angel's house, shouting, hurling abuse, throwing stones and smashing windows. Angel picked up his shotgun loaded with bird shot and went out to send the mob away. Almost the instant he passed through the door Angel shouldered the gun and fired. John Grange received most of the shot in his stomach, killing him.

Angel was brought before Huntingdon Assizes. In his summing up the learned judge was keen to emphasise the difference between wilful murder, 'the symptom of a wicked and depraved mind and of a heart regardless of social duty, and fatally bent upon mischief' and manslaughter, an act committed 'under the influence of strong provocation' to the jury. They returned a verdict of 'manslaughter'. Angel was sentenced to be transported for life.

John Bishop was not so lucky; at the same assizes he was found guilty of stealing twenty sheep, the property of Mr T. Lindsell of Hemingford Grey. Bishop was sentenced to death.

7 SEPTEMBER 1883

A Foulmere servant girl was removed to Addenbrooke's Hospital suffering from paralysis, the result of a practical joke. She had gone to the larder of the house where she was employed and a man's hand appeared moving back and forth at the top of a partition. She became so alarmed at the sight because she could discern no body attached to the hand it brought on the paralysis. The girl did survive, but was rendered speechless.

8 SEPTEMBER 1727

Puppeteer Robert Shepheard, his family and retinue were passing through Burwell on their way to Stourbridge Fair. They thought it would be a good village to raise a few funds for their coffers by performing one of their shows. They hired a barn situated near Cockles Row from Mr Wosson and set about publicising their event. Folk came from many of the surrounding villages to pay their penny and see the show. The barn was filled to capacity, and the audience numbered well over 100, some of them even sat on the beams. To ensure no one could subsequently sneak in without a ticket, the doors were 'nailed shut'. The Burwell parish register records:

> At about 9 o'clock on the evening of September 8th 1727, fire broke out in a barn, in which a great number of persons were met together to see a puppet show. In the barn were a great many loads of new light straw. The barn was thatched with straw which was very dry, and the inner roof was covered with old dry cobwebs, so that the fire like lightening flew around the barn in an instant. There was but one small door, which was close nailed up, and could not easily be broken down. When it was opened, the passage was so narrow and everybody so impatient to escape that the door was presently blocked up, and most of those that did escape, which was but very few, were forced to crawl over

The stone marking the mass grave of the victims of the puppet show fire, Burwell churchyard.

the bodies of those that lay in a heap by the door. Seventy six perished immediately and two more died of their wounds within two days.

First on the scene was Wicken man Thomas Dobedee, 'a stout man in the prime of life.' Dobedee led the effort pulling people from the fire; he risked his life and his hair was singed. The wind fanned the flames, the fire spread to five nearby houses, burning them to the ground, and claiming the life of bed-bound Mary Woodbridge in the process. After half an hour the thatched roof of the barn collapsed and any hope of more rescues was lost. In such rural communities it was hardly surprising that every local family was touched by the disaster.

The cause of the fire was, at the time, claimed to have been a candle set in a lantern near a heap of straw by servant Richard Whitaker. Tried at the assizes, he was acquitted from the charge of arson although criticised for his negligence. A stone carved with a flaming heart was erected over the graves of the victims in the churchyard.

A curious postscript to this story was reported in the *Cambridge Chronicle* in February 1774. An old man who had died a few days previously in Fordham said he had a 'burthen on his Mind which he must disclose.' He then confessed that he had set fire to the barn at Burwell because he harboured 'an antipathy to the Puppet Show Man.' The man was not named, but rumours abounded that the confession came during the near-death delirium of Richard Whitaker.

9 SEPTEMBER 1928

The *Sunday Chronicle* published a short account of Mother Redcap of Horseheath, who died in 1926:

> One day a black man called, produced a book, and asked her to sign her name in it. The women signed the book, and the mysterious stranger then told her she would be the mistress of five imps who would carry out her orders. Shortly afterwards the woman was seen out accompanied by a rat, a cat, a toad, a ferret and a mouse. Everybody believed she was a witch and many people visited her to obtain cures.

10 SEPTEMBER 1800

Ann Hyson, 'a poor woman of Cambridge', complained to the vice-chancellor that, having taken her gleanings to be ground at one of the windmills in Chesterton field, the miller, instead of returning her own flour, gave her nothing but that of refuse wheat. The vice-chancellor caused the miller to be immediately apprehended; found the case as stated and insisted on giving the poor woman a guinea before he left the Lodge.

11 SEPTEMBER 1848

The following advertisement appeared in the local paper:

> Staff required for Ely Union Workhouse. The Guardians give notice, that at their adjourned board meeting to be held on Thursday 21st of September instant, at 10 o'clock, they will be prepared to receive and decide on applications for the respective situations of Master, Matron, Schoolmaster, Schoolmistress and Porter of the Union Workhouse at Ely now vacant. The salary of the Master and Matron will be £30 per annum: for the schoolmaster £25: schoolmistress £20 and the Porter £20: with board and lodgings in the workhouse.

The candidates will be expected to possess a competent knowledge of the duties of their respective offices and must attend personally at the meeting, with testimonials of character and fitness. The duties to commence at Michaelmas. The Guardians do not pledge themselves to appoint any of the candidates and it should be distinctly understood that no person can be appointed to any of the above offices who does not agree to give one month's notice previous to resigning the office, or to forfeit one month's amount of salary.

12 SEPTEMBER John Howard Reports on the Prisons of Cambridgeshire & Huntingdon

Wisbech Bridewell and Gaol, 1782:

There is a descent of 5 steps. Two rooms below (the work room is 15 feet by 12), and two above. No Court: no water accessible to prisoners. Allowance, a penny a day: straw, twenty shillings a year. Clauses of act against spirituous liquors, and the act for preserving the health of prisoners not hung up. Keeper's salary, £16: no fees – This prison might be improved on the keeper's garden.

13 SEPTEMBER 1740

Thomas Higgins and William Organer were hanged 'as a warning to others' at Wisbech for their role as ringleaders during the corn riot in the town the previous month. The mob had attacked a number of buildings and warehouses, smashing windows and even pulled one house down entirely. A number of granaries were entered by force; three or four were opened with keys after the mob intimidated the owners. A total of twenty last of wheat were carried off and several gentlemen and tradesmen had money extracted from them by the mob. The rioters sold the wheat at 1d a bushelm, but the bulk they carried home to their own houses. The damage caused by the riot was thought at the time to be to the value of £500–£600.

14 SEPTEMBER 1791

James Boutell (32) was brought before the Common Sergeant at the Old Bailey on the indictment that he had married Catherine Watts on 3 March 1776 in the parish of Great Seaford, but then deserted her, left for London and took up with another woman named Elizabeth Vanhagen, whom he also married, on 28 May 1788, in the parish of St Sepulchre. John Scott, the parish clerk of Great Shelford, was brought to the court with his register books. He had known both James Boutell and Catherine Watts; he was even present at their wedding and testified he recalled Boutell leaving about four years previously. When asked by the judge what he had to say to the charge, Boutell replied, 'I liked the girl [Vanhagen] very well, and did not like the first; and I thought no crime in it.' Found guilty of bigamy, Boutell was fined 1s and imprisoned for twelve months.

15 SEPTEMBER Grim sayings of Cambridgeshire

Sutton for mutton
Potton for beef
Gamblingay for pretty girls
Waresley for thieves.

The Needingworth fire hooks, used for pulling down burning thatch, can be seen on display on a wall in Needingworth High Street.

16 SEPTEMBER 1847

Serious fire at Needingworth. At about 12 noon a servant girl foolishly threw some lighted straw into a yard, the high winds prevalent on that day caught hold of it and carried it onto the thatch of a nearby cottage, setting it on fire. The fire soon spread to nearby houses and farms. A number of the local fire engines attended the scene, but, it was reported, 'in consequence of the wind and scarcity of water were quite useless.' When the fire was eventually extinguished a total of eighty-six houses had been destroyed and many others damaged. The ruins of the burnt village proved to be a great draw for sightseers and soon a subscription was raised to provide some money for those who suffered loss in the fire.

17 SEPTEMBER 1783

Thomas Eaton was executed at Littleport. Tried at the Wisbech Assizes, Eaton had been found guilty of setting fire to the barns of his employer, Mr Tansley. Eaton swore he was innocent and died with the exclamation 'Gentlemen I die innocent' upon his lips.

18 SEPTEMBER 1663

Diarist Samuel Pepys leaves Parson Drove. He had arrived the previous day to visit his uncle, aunt and their family. Pepys wrote of his visit in his diary:

Samuel Pepys.

I begun a journey, with much ado, through the fens, along dikes, where sometimes we were ready to have our horses sink to the belly, we got by night with a great deal of stir, and hard riding to Parson Drove, a heathen place, where I found my uncle and aunt Perkins and their daughters, poor wretches, in a sad, poor thatched cottage, like a poor barn, or stable, peeling of hemp and in a poor condition of habitt took them to our miserable inne.

While at the inn, the Swan, the group entertained themselves, Frank the miller played his treble and they sat down to supper. News came that one of the groups' horses had been stolen out of the stable, Pepys was glad it was not his. He continued:

... so about twelve at night or more, to bed in a sad, cold, nasty chamber, only the mayde was indifferent handsome, and so I had a kiss or two of her, and I to bed, and a little after I was asleep they waked me to tell me that the horse was found, which was good newes, and so to sleep till the morning, but was bit cruelly, and nobody else of our company, which I wonder at, by the gnatts.

19 SEPTEMBER 1847

Incendiary fire reported at Trumpington Hall, the seat of Colonel Pemberton. A messenger had been sent to summon the appliances from a number of different fire offices in Cambridge and within half an hour they were on the scene and in action. Upon arrival however, they found it was not the hall that was on fire but some nearby hay stacks. There were some thirty stacks in the vicinity, but the arsonist had started the fire at the end where the wind carried the fire away from the rest of the stacks and Trumpington village. The supply of water was good, plenty of people came to assist and the fire was subdued, but not without the loss of three corn stacks and some haul-stacks.

20 SEPTEMBER 1940

Two parachutists glide silently down onto Fen Field near Globe Farm on the outskirts of Willingham. Intercepted by the local Home Guard, they were both arrested. Both were Nazi spies who had been dropped on England to gather information that may have been of use for the impending invasion. One of them was Wulf Schmidt; he had been dropped in Danish Army uniform, with both Danish and British identity papers (in the name of Harold Williamson) and £132 in cash. The plan had been that the pair pass themselves off as Danish soldiers until a better cover could be established.

Once in captivity, Schmidt was given the choice of becoming a double agent or be hanged as a spy. On 16 October 1940 he transmitted his first dud message to his spymasters in Germany. Over the course of the war he sent over a thousand carefully crafted, misleading and deceitful messages. After the war he thought it best to remain in Britain and this he did, as Harry Williamson.

21 SEPTEMBER

Reports were published of the inquest held at the Union Workhouse, Cambridge, before Mr C.F. Jarrold, deputy coroner, upon the body of Mr William Leeland, a gardener. The evidence presented told how Leeland and his friend, Mr Giddings, were walking on the 4ft way of the railway near Cambridge railway station when the train from Wisbech arrived. The two men crossed the metals of the Newmarket line, where there was no public footpath, and were making their way to the platform when both men were knocked down by the Wisbech train travelling at about 6mph.

Leeland was fearfully mutilated, his right leg and arm were severed from his body and he died instantly. Giddings was conveyed to hospital and at the time of the inquest was making good progress. The jury returned a verdict of 'accidental death', adding no blame was to be attached to the train crew.

22 SEPTEMBER 1825

The Association for the Prosecution of all kinds of Felony within the Hundred of Ely and South-part of the Hundred of Witchford publish a poster seeking information about 'nine shearling wethers, fresh in condition, marked with the letter 'V' on the rump, with pitch' belonging to Mr Benjamin Vipan and thought to have been stolen or strayed from the ground known as 'Skeel's Hundred' near Welch's Dam in the Isle of Ely. The clue to the cause of their disappearance was noted on the poster, 'A man was seen driving a small quantity of sheep near the above place between 11 and 12 o'clock at night on which same were lost.' A reward of 10 guineas was offered to whoever could give such information which would convict the offender or offenders. If the sheep were found to have strayed, the person who returned them would be rewarded for his trouble.

23 SEPTEMBER 1885

Mr Peckham of Acacia Road, St John's Wood was with two companions at Welney for two days fishing. While returning by a shortcut up the Great Eastern Railway line near March, the Doncaster express dashed past. Mr Peckham appeared to step back and was drawn under the train. He was dreadfully mutilated and died shortly after his arrival at the Peterborough Infirmary.

24 SEPTEMBER 1652

The execution took place of the notorious Royalist highwayman Captain James Hind (34). To keep one step ahead of the law, Hind had worked over some considerable area of southern England and always took a great pleasure in robbing Parliamentarians.

Hind and another 'Knight of the High Toby' named Tom Allen had the chance to raid the Lord Protector himself when he was travelling from Huntingdon to London on the Great North Road. No doubt aware this road was an infamous haunt of highwaymen, Cromwell had no less than seven men in his train. Our highwaymen sighted the coach about a mile south of Godmanchester and blocked the road ahead with their horses. Cromwell's riders could see what was afoot and were swift and well-rehearsed in their reaction. The Captain of the Guard fired his musket first, hitting Allen in the leg; the blast threw him from his saddle. Hind was not going to hang around and rode off at breakneck speed amid a hail of musket shots. Allen was arrested and escorted to Cambridge where his wounds were dressed. He was tried for highway robbery and implicated Hind, but this did not save his skin – he was found guilty and was hanged.

Hind had ridden so hard to get out of danger after this encounter with Cromwell that he killed his horse, and he had not at that time money enough to buy another. So, to procure one as soon as possible he tramped along the road on foot. It was not long before he saw a horse tied to a hedge with a brace of pistols before him; and looking round him, he observed on the other side of the hedge a gentleman un trussing a point. Hind shouted 'This is my horse' and immediately vaulted into the saddle. The gentleman shouted to him, that the horse was his. 'Sir,' replied Hind, 'you may think yourself well off that I have left you all the money in your pockets to buy another, which you had best lay out before I meet you again, lest you should be worse used.'

Hide was eventually captured and by an Order of Council he was removed by *habeas corpus* to Worcester jail. At the beginning of September 1652, he was condemned for high treason. On the 24 September Hind was hanged, drawn and quartered. It was said gold coins he had swallowed for concealment fell from his guts as they were opened. After the execution Hind's head was set upon the Bridge Gate, over the River Severn, from whence it was privately taken down and buried within a week afterwards. His limbs were put upon the other gates of the city, where they remained till they were destroyed by wind and weather.

25 SEPTEMBER 1842

Reports circulate of 'an extraordinary attempt at murder' made by James Mallers (or Mallard) upon his wife at Hemingford. On the previous Sunday afternoon, when most were away from the house he shared with his father-in-law, Mallers enticed his pregnant wife to a well in the back part of the premises, and as soon as she appeared distracted he seized her and threw her down the 12ft shaft of the well. In the fall her head remained upwards and as there was only about 5ft of water in the well she was able to keep her mouth above the water. The report in *The Times* stated:

> Seeing that his object was not likely to be effected, the murderous wretch jumped down upon her shoulders and endeavoured to trample her under the water. During this attempt the struggles of the woman for life were dreadful; and each time that her head rose above the surface she made use of the brief breathing space to beseech him in the most agonising tones to spare her.

Highwayman Captain James Hind claims another victim.

The murderous cove replied he had 'gone too far to stop' and she would surely hang him if he spared her life. Moved at last by either pity or fear of discovery, he relented and got a ladder, helped her out and she went to her bedroom. He tried to get in the room, but she had had the presence of mind to lock the door and her husband saw his chance to make his escape. Her deposition was taken down and a warrant issued for the apprehension of her husband, who was supposed to have fled to London.

26 SEPTEMBER 1825

The annual Stirbitch Horse Fair was commenced. Also known as 'Sturbritch' and a few unprintables, these colloquial names for Stourbridge Fair hint something of the ribaldry there. The fair dated back to 1199, when King John granted the Leper Chapel at Steresbrigge in Cambridge a dispensation to hold a three-day fair to raise money to support the lepers. Held from 1211 around the Feast of the Holy Cross (14 September) on the open land of Stourbridge Common alongside the River Cam, by the sixteenth century records indicate vulgar and indecent behaviour at this event.

*Jacob Butler, Master
of Sturbridge Fair.*

In 1547 a complaint from the civic authorities involved prisoners, taken by the proctors of the university, in the last Sturbridge fair for 'naughty and corrupt behaviour.' By the seventeenth century, coaches were bringing revellers from all over the eastern counties, hackney-coaches even made the journey from London.

A notorious fair required a great character to maintain it, and in the eighteenth century that man was Jacob Butler Esq., a barrister-at-law who lived at Abbey House, Barnwell. A contemporary account recorded:

> In stature he was six feet four inches high, of determined character, and deemed a great eccentric because, among other reasons, he usually invited the giants and dwarfs, who came for exhibition, to dine with him. He was so rigid in seeing the charter literally complied with, that if the ground was not cleared by one o'clock on the day appointed, and he found any of the booths standing, he had them pulled down, and the materials taken away. On one occasion when the wares were not removed by the time mentioned in the charter, he drove his carriage among the crockery and destroyed a great quantity.

27 SEPTEMBER 1888

William Snelling, the master brewer at Messrs Jenkins and Jones's brewery in Huntingdon, had been shooting and returned, with his gun, to attend to his duties at the brewery for the afternoon. At about 3.45 p.m. Snelling was in the mash room where David Wombwell and John Tuck were boiling stout, filling the room with noise and steam. Snelling sent Tuck up a ladder into the copper room to take sample of the stout. Within a few minutes Snelling was heard crying out 'For God's sake, help,' witnesses conflicted over if they heard a gunshot before or after the cries. Alfred Coldham the cooper rushed upstairs and found Snelling lying across the doorway, bleeding from the nose and mouth and unable to speak; he had been shot in the back and he died about fifteen minutes later without regaining speech.

Enquiries revealed there was some 'ill-will' between Snelling and Wombwell, so David Wombwell was taken into custody and charged with his murder. At the trial, Alfred Coldham claimed he saw Wombwell standing nearby with a gun in his hands; it was pointing towards where Snelling lay. Coldham 'caught hold' of the gun, Wombwell let go of it and he set it down on the side of the mash tub. As more people came into the room, Coldham thought the gun looked dangerous where it lay so he picked it up to move it to safety, but as he did so the other charge exploded and went into the floor.

Mr Grain for the defence was quick to point out that Coldham had said nothing about Wombwell holding the gun at the inquest and an open verdict had been recorded. Other witnesses were called, who stated another worker named Livet had said he had moved the gun, no other witnesses said they saw Wombwell hold or even touch the weapon; in fact the only evidence against Wombwell were a few 'suspicious statements' allegedly made by him to various persons that were easily dismissed by his able defence barrister, indeed, as it was reported, 'Mr Grain launched the case against Wombwell into a sea of doubt.' After a careful summing up by Mr Justice Mathew, the jury retired and almost immediately returned a verdict of 'not guilty.'

28 SEPTEMBER 1803

Posters offering a reward of 100 guineas were put up around Cambridge seeking those who had raised a false cry of 'fire' at Stourbridge Fair theatre (a deed thought to have been committed by rogues with the object of plunder). Although managers and performers tried every persuasion to calm the crowd, a panic erupted. Several people scrambled down or threw themselves from the upper boxes and gallery into the pit. Some fell down the gallery stairs and in the rush to get out, many were injured and Rose Mason (24), Mary Freeman (13), Esther Cook (12) and John Smith (14) were all trampled to death. The culprits escaped detection.

29 SEPTEMBER Punishments of the Past: Branding

In September 1713 the Ordinary of Newgate Prison, London recorded the list of those executed upon this day at Tyburn. Among them was:

> Thomas Turner, condemn'd for stealing a brown Gelding, out of the Ground of Mr Ambrose Benning, on the 20th Day of August last. He said, he was 30 Years of Age, born at Thriplow in Cambridgeshire: That his chief Employment was Husbandry; but had made it part of his Trade for these six Years past to steal Sheep and Hogs, and was for such a Fact burnt in the Hand at Cambridge about nine Months ago.

Being 'burnt in the Hand' alludes to branding, a punishment carried out by the application of a red-hot branding iron to the hand or face. The letter you were branded with depended on your crime and gave a good idea of the types of criminal acts that carried this horrible punishment: 'V' for vagabond, 'T' for thief, 'C' for coin-clipper,

Administering a red-hot brand to a convicted felon.

'B' for Blasphemer, 'SS' (one 'S' either side of the nose) for those who sowed sedition, 'M' for malefactors, 'FA' for false accuser.

In 1726 prisoners who could demonstrate their ability to 'read like a clerk' were not treated as common criminals but had the right to be cold ironed whereby, on payment of a small sum, the branding iron was plunged into cold water before being pressed against the skin.

30 SEPTEMBER 1905

The last fraud was committed by George H. Young (26), who claimed to be a clerk by trade; he was in reality a serial thief and swindler. He had been dismissed from the Army with ignominy, but forged an honourable discharge, then obtained a situation as a clerk by forgery. Using the railways to flit from place to place, he stole two watches at Leeds, another at York then a number of travelling cases from London stations, he even stole a suit worth £2 10s at Great Yarmouth. Attiring himself in good clothes, he assumed a number of identities and obtained trust by deception.

In his last fraud, conducted at Cambridge between 25 and 30 September, he posed as Lieutenant Murphy, whose property he had stolen at Euston railway station. During the time he was in the city he unlawfully incurred a debt of £4 1s 6d. Brought before the assizes, he pleaded 'guilty' on all counts. The learned judge, in passing sentence, said that he thought that not only the county of Cambridge but all England were much indebted to Detective Marsh for capturing 'one of the cleverest swindlers and scoundrels.' Concluding the prisoner 'was one of those men who should be kept in prison, if not for the rest of his life, at any rate a long time', the judge sentenced him to seven years' penal servitude.

OCTOBER

The historic Firmary Lane in the precincts of Ely Cathedral. The ghostly figures of monks have been seen here at night on numerous occasions.

1 OCTOBER 1785

Charles Collignon dies. He had been Professor of Anatomy at Cambridge University and had been described by William Cole, a contemporary, as 'a most suitable person for the position, as he is a walking skeleton himself.' Collignon regularly conducted a course of twenty-eight lectures during the Lent term at the anatomy amphitheatre on Queens' Lane opposite the entrance to Queen's College and close to Silver Street. The bodies he used for his dissections were often obtained from resurrectionists.

In March 1768 the body on the table caused a stir, before he realised it himself a number of students recognised it as the corpse of Laurence Sterne, the author of *The Life and Opinions of Tristram Shandy*, who had died of consumption and had been buried in the new burial ground of St George's, Hanover Square only a couple of days previously. The anatomisation was carried out, but it appears Collignon was concerned about the fate of the body and being found out as a man who used the services of bodysnatchers, so he had it sent back to London for a discreet reburial.

When the churchyard of St George's was redeveloped in the 1960s, Sterne's skull was disinterred (in a manner befitting the man who enjoyed his nickname of 'Yorick') and was identified by the fact that it was the only skull of the five in Sterne's grave that bore evidence of having been anatomised. It was transferred to its final resting place in Coxwold churchyard, North Yorkshire in 1969.

The anatomised skull of an executed felon.

2 OCTOBER Report of the Prison Inspectors

Cambridge County Gaol, 1853:

> Number of Prisoners at time of Inspection: 42 Males, 9 Debtors (Female Prisoners are sent to the Town Gaol).
>
> I found the buildings in good order: the ventilation and drainage good. Alterations to the infirmary had been made and the sinks for washing removed from the day rooms, as recommended by the last inspection; six cells have been fitted and certified for separate confinement for limited periods; eight other cells are being altered for the same purpose. There has been no adulteration in the diet, clothing or bedding. The provisions were of good quality; the daily cost for food was 3½d per head.
>
> The general health of the prisoners has been good; there had been one death (from epilepsy) and three prisoners had been liberated on medical grounds, all three consumptive patients under sentence for long periods. In neither case was the disease apparent when the prisoners were admitted. There has been no change in the duties performed by the chaplain ... The chaplain considers the progress made by the prisoners to be equal to what may be 'reasonably expected' – On admission, out of a total of 305 prisoners 113 could neither read nor write, 120 could read only, 70 could read and write

imperfectly and only 2 could read and write well … The conduct of the prisoners was 'generally good.' The number of punishments for prison offences was 56; the most severe punishment, confinement in a light cell for three days on bread and water.

The treadwheel was not at work when I inspected the prison, but all the prisoners were fully employed. Most of the prisoners received in this gaol are agricultural labourers, and being committed for short periods there is little or no work done for sale. The estimated value of work done by prisoners for the prison was £154 5s 10d. I examined the journals and other books; they were all entered up to the day of my visit and the accounts appear to be properly kept.

Both the Governor and the Chaplain of the gaol report favourably of the separate system, so far as it is carried out in the prison. The chaplain recommends that it may be extended as far as practicable; and in his report to the magistrates he says: 'Separate confinement is in reality the only regulation in this prison that deserves the name of discipline.' The Governor says: 'It is desirable, on account of its deterring effect, that as many cells as the nature of the building will admit of should be adapted for carrying out the separate system.' Out of the 305 criminals committed during the year 250 were placed in separate confinement in the 22 cells already certified. The cells are small, and have therefore only been certified for periods not exceeding one month. In no case has any prisoner been kept in separate confinement for a period exceeding 28 days. The ventilations of the cells is good. The thermometer stood at 60° when I inspected the prison, and it was not lower than 55° during the preceding winter.

3 OCTOBER 1789

A report in the *Cambridge Chronicle* stated that an inquest had been held into the death of an Irishman who had died after a fight with John Page of Littleport. The jury returned a verdict of 'manslaughter' against Page, but he had already absconded.

4 OCTOBER 1892

Concerns spread through March after local potato merchant Mr J. Harlow had reportedly died from cholera. Dr Waters, the medical officer of health for the district, called Dr T.J. Walker of Peterborough for a second opinion. He confirmed the diagnosis. The matter was reported to the Local Government Board and all the clothing of the deceased were burned as a precaution against contamination. Further examination of Mr Harlow resulted in a medical certificate issued for his death being caused by severe choleraic diarrhoea (also known as summer diarrhoea – acute gastroenteritis due to bacterial infection). The fear and suspicion that 'King Cholera' could have returned to the town would not easily abate so the board inspector directed a number of precautionary measures be put in place and advised the free use of disinfectants across the town.

5 OCTOBER 1570

The English chronicler Raphael Holinshed recorded on this date:

> A terrible tempest of winde and raine, the sea break in betwixt Wisbech and Walsoken and at the Cross Keies, drowning Tilnie and old Lin, Saint Marie Tid, St Johns Walpole, Walton and Walsoken, Emneie, Jarmans and Stowbridge all being the space of ten miles.

A wayward prisoner in the Refractory Cell. Prisoners could be punished this way for transgressions such as fighting, temper or disobedience. They were kept in total darkness, fed just ½lb of bread morning and evening and given only water to drink.

6 OCTOBER 1681

After performing his services on or about this day, the Capital Burgesses of Wisbech:

> Ordered Mr William Neave to be allowed the sume of Three Pounds on his perfect Curinge A sore legg or Margery Upcraft; but in case noe cure no allowance; the money to be paid in the Cure, But in case ye distemper break out in 12 months Mr Neave to cure itt again or repay 30s to the Burgesses.

7 OCTOBER Grim Tales of Cambridgeshire: 'The Dirtiest Place I Ever Saw'

Celia Fiennes, the daughter of a Roundhead colonel, travelled around England on horseback between 1684 and about 1712 'to regain my health by variety and change of aire and exercise', recording her experiences and thoughts of where she visited as she went along. At this time the idea of travel for its own sake was still quite novel, and women travelling – as Lady Celia did, with only a couple of servants – over long distances was very rare. When she visited Ely in 1695 she recorded the only way into the city was by a causeway that was flooded in winter. She was alarmed when her horse nearly tipped into the flooded dyke beside this causeway when it reached down to drink. Fiennes described Ely as 'the dirtiest place I ever saw, not a bit of pitching in the streets except round the Palace and the churches. The Bishop does not care to stay long in this place not being for his health.' Of the local men she said, 'they are slothful people and for little but the taking care of their grounds and cattle.'

8 OCTOBER 1892

Mind your language! Major Frank Fisher of the King's Own Scottish Borderers was brought before the Cambridge Police Court. Major Fisher had recently appeared on charges of using threatening language to his wife, this time he was charged with using obscene language in St Andrew's Street, which he strenuously denied and threatened to bring his 'harsh treatment' at the hands of the local police to the notice of his relative, Colonel Howard Vincent. Unmoved by such bluster the magistrates were satisfied PC Perry and a number of witnesses spoke the truth and, finding the major guilty, sentenced him to fourteen days' imprisonment – without hard labour. Major Fisher asked if he could pay a fine instead. The Bench stuck with a committal and Major Fisher was taken down as he attempted to prevaricate and demand an appeal.

9 OCTOBER 1868

High winds cause damage across Great Britain. A reported 'hurricane' swept across Cambridgeshire, demolishing a number of barns, and uprooting many mature trees, and carried the wreckage over some considerable distance.

10 OCTOBER 1804

A disturbance caused by about 3,000 French prisoners of war was staged at Norman Cross. *The Times* stated:

> An incessant uproar was kept up all morning and at noon their intention to attempt the destruction of the barriers of the prison became so obvious that the Commanding Officer, apprehensive that the force under his command, consisting of only Shropshire Militia, and one Battalion of the Army of Reserve would not be sufficient, in case of extremity, to environ and restrain so large a body of prisoners.

He sent a messenger requesting assistance from the Volunteer Force in Peterborough, fortunately they were having a field day and a troop was able to attend immediately upon the arrival of the messenger. The tumult continued until nightfall, when a number of French prisoners attempted to escape. Further reinforcements were requested from Peterborough along with two additional troops of Yeomanry. The prisoners did succeed in cutting down part of the wood enclosure during the night and nine escaped. As soon as daylight broke it was discovered they had under mined a distance of 34ft towards the great south road, under the fosse which surrounded the prison. This had not been excavated enough to enable escape. Within a very short period five of the nine escaped prisoners were recaptured.

11 OCTOBER 1757

John Freeman was executed on the Ely gallows after being tried and found guilty of the murder of Joseph Stott.

12 OCTOBER 1804

Cambridge was troubled by a mysterious 'fiery spirit' whose 'pranks' included the sending of a 'sudden gust' of fiery flame up the skirts and upon the stockings of a number of servant girls. Strange glowing lights were also observed floating around the town. It was suggested that these manifestations could have been caused by a build up of gases underground. *The Times* was convinced the escapades of the 'fiery spirit' would 'become the subject of a new play or novel for the delight and terror of the spectre-loving circles, who are by no means the least numerous amongst the votaries of curiosity.'

13 OCTOBER 1877

Clara Reddan (21), daughter of a grocer at Murrow, died from the effects of strychnine. Before death she declared she was pregnant by a man named Shotcliffe, her sister's husband, who had given her a powder to do her good. At the inquest, held in Wisbech, the jury returned a verdict of 'death from strychnine, but how administered there was not sufficient evidence to show.'

14 OCTOBER 1909

Lily Parsons (23) was brought before the Cambridge Assizes charged with wounding Harry Norfield with a knife at Chesterton on 14 September. Parsons pleaded 'guilty'; she had been engaged to Norfield, but after 'some information had reached him as to her character' (perhaps he found out she had already had at least one, some suggested two, children out of wedlock) he broke it off and both he and his mother wrote her letters to the effect.

On the day in question Norfield was working in a field with another man when Parsons, having walked the 16 miles from Ely, 'suddenly appeared from a hedge' and stabbed Norfield in the back. An ex-police sergeant happened to be nearby and took charge of the girl; the knife was found in her left-hand glove and she claimed Norfield had 'got her into trouble,' now he would have nothing to do with her and after her mother had seen the letters from Norfield and his mother she had been turned out of her house and had had no food for two days. In fact, Lily Parsons had left a letter for her mother in which she said she was going to take revenge by killing Norfield then commit suicide. As the letters were read in court Parsons became violent and angry. The Deputy Chief Constable stated Parsons had been dismissed by three employers because of her intemperate outbursts. She was sentenced to six months with hard labour.

15 OCTOBER 1835

Charles Brand (76), of Elsworth, committed suicide by hanging himself. At the inquest the tragic story behind this deed was told. Seven years previously Mr Brand had the good fortune to have been left the sum of £100. Perhaps being advanced in years he never thought he could spend all that money in the years he had left so he decided to enjoy it while he could; perhaps he was just no good with money. Either way a week previous to his suicide he changed his last sovereign, and apparently the prospect of being obliged to resort to the parish for relief seemed to have had such an effect upon his mind 'already enfeebled by years' that it caused him to take his own life. The jury returned a verdict of 'lunacy'.

16 OCTOBER 1869

A report was published stating that Frederick Fincham (18), the Littleport arsonist, had been apprehended for firing a stack, the property of Mr H.W. Martin. Found guilty of the crime at the assizes, Fincham was sentenced to five years' penal servitude. Just three or four decades earlier he would certainly have been hanged for the same crime. Curiously, when Fincham had been behind bars a few months, another fire was discovered, again in the farmyard of Mr H.W. Martin.

17 OCTOBER 1878

The Revd Robert Watson Rowson, vicar of Aylesby, Lincolnshire, was convicted at the Peterborough Quarter Sessions of stealing an overcoat from an eating house in Peterborough. He was sentenced to three months' imprisonment with hard labour.

18 OCTOBER 1845

Revd R. Yeatman recorded his impression of the St Ives workhouse, Huntingdon:

> I saw sitting on wooden benches in front of their bastille, and within their ring wall and its railings, some half hundred or more of these men; tall, robust figures, young mostly or of middle age, of honest countenance, many of them thoughtful and even intelligent looking men. They sat there, nearby one another; but in a kind of torpor, especially in silence which was very striking ... in the eyes and brows of these men hung the gloomiest expression, not of anger but of grief and shame, and manifold inarticulate distress and weariness; they returned my glance with a glance that seemed to say 'Don't look at us. We sit enchanted here, we know not why. The sun shines and the earth calls; and by the governing powers and impotences of this England we are forbidden to obey. It is impossible they tell us.' There was something that reminded me of Dante's Hell in the look of all this, and I rode swiftly away.

19 OCTOBER Report of the Prison Inspectors

Wisbech House of Correction, 1853:

> Number of Prisoners at time of Inspection: 26 Males 9 Females.
>
> No alterations have been made either in the buildings or in the discipline of the prison since the last inspection but the drainage was about to be improved. The ventilation is good. There has been one death; a prisoner who died from abscess on the side. The general health of the prisoners was represented to be good. There was one prisoner, a female, sick at the time of my visit.
>
> There is still no regular schoolmaster; but the Governor instructs the male prisoners and last year received a gratuity of £15 for this extra duty. The number of punishments

for prison offences was – males 299, females 14. They were generally for talking, idleness or want of cleanliness. Some prisoners are still employed sorting oats but in addition to the making and repairing of prison clothes and shoes, sack making has been introduced. The clear profits on receipts for this kind of work was £8 15s 6d. The estimated value of work done for the prison was £27 14s 9d. All the provisions, fuel and other stores are supplied by contract. The net cost per prisoner, exclusive of any charge for repairs etc, was £26 10s 4d. I again called the attention of the visiting justices to the absence of any artificial light in the cells; the prisoners are locked up at dusk, and continue to pass much time in bed.

The practice of eating opium is indulged to a great extent in this district. One woman, who had been accustomed to take extraordinary quantities before she came to prison, felt the deprivation so keenly that she made an attempt to destroy herself. She had been some time in the prison when I saw her and expressed herself as feeling very thankful for having been broken of the habit, though she represented the deprivation as having, at first, 'almost made her mad.'

The prisoners generally are of a very low standard, both as regard morals and intellect, this in some measure attributed to the free use of this drug. I found one prisoner who had been 27 times in this gaol. He is represented to be a quite well-disposed man, until he is either drunk or under the influence of opium.

20 OCTOBER Strange Tales and Folklore of Cambridgeshire: Last of the Lumpkins

One family name associated for generations with Tydd St Giles, especially in the seventeenth and eighteenth centuries, is that of the Lumpkins. One story attached to them relates to John Lumpkin, the last of the line. When his father died John was only left a shilling – so he gave it to some travelling players to go and dance on the old man's grave. John's own sad end came when he fell from a wagon while drunk, his body was passed over by the wheels and thus ended the life of poor John Lumpkin.

The prison workroom, where prisoners repaired and made prison clothes.

21 OCTOBER 1853

A cholera outbreak was reported in Soham. The *Cambridge Chronicle* stated:

> A poor man named Bye called upon H. Miller Esq., surgeon, to make a small payment to the Medical Club of which he was a member. He was in perfect health; about an hour afterwards he became alarmingly ill and Mr Miller pronounced symptoms of Asiatic Cholera. The man died at 3 o'clock in the morning, the hands having the same shrivelled appearance as a washer woman's. Four fresh cases of cholera developed last Wednesday and more cases of diarrhoea. A boy was also buried last week.

The report from the General Board of Health dated 31 October stated:

> Ten deaths from cholera and two from diarrhoea are reported as having occurred in Soham since the 21st October, six from cholera and one from diarrhoea happened within the last 30 hours prior to the despatch of the latest accounts. Upwards of 40 cases (some very severe in their character) occurred on the 30th alone. From 120 to 130 cases of choleraic diarrhoea are stated to have taken place in various parts of the district. Dr Lewis has been directed by the General Board of Health to visit the locality immediately, to advice with Local authorities as to the adoption of precautionary measures.

22 OCTOBER 1816

Reports were published of the recent Quarter Sessions for Cambridge. The notable cases included the Revd Thomas Finch, who was found guilty of assaulting Elizabeth Benton and duly sentenced to a week in the town gaol and fined £10. The case of two young farmers from Upwell, namely John Lister and J. Vulpuym, was also heard. They were found guilty of 'riotously assaulting Joseph Scott, a respectable farmer of the same parish' and sentenced to two months' imprisonment.

23 OCTOBER 1848

A suspected murder by poison occurred at Old Weston. An extraordinary degree of excitement prevailed in the village following the allegations of a servant who, having been dismissed after years of loyal service, revealed that local lady Mrs Parsons, who had recently re-married, had in fact killed her first husband, Mr James Smith, the previous year. Local people could remember Smith as a fit and healthy man of temperate habits; his illness had been as violent as it was sudden. Smith had been seized with violent retching and purging and had suffered 'the most frightful agony' until he died. Mr Beedham the coroner ordered an exhumation of the body and committed it to Messrs Peck and Fernie, surgeons of Kimbolton, and Mr Foster of Huntingdon for post-mortem examination.

24 OCTOBER 1795

Itinerant Irish farm labourers James Culley, Michael Quin, Thomas Quin and Thomas Markin were hanged at Wisbech after being tried and found guilty of entering the home of shepherd William Marriot on Wisbech High Fen, where they brutally assaulted and killed Mr Marriott, his wife and a young lodger. They then made off with a few items of jewellery, silver spoons, a little money and a coat. Apprehended in Staffordshire, many of the items they had robbed from the house were found about their persons. Tried and found guilty, the four were executed before a large crowd. After being left to 'swing' for an hour the bodies were then cut down. The bodies of Markin and Thomas Quinn were delivered to the surgeons while the bodies of James Culley and Michael Quinn were hung in chains from a gibbet on the north bank of Morton's Leam.

25 OCTOBER 1903

Mr Phillip Draycott of Wisbech, his wife, their eight-year-old son and a family friend named Green were driving back home from Crowland to Wisbech in a storm. Mr Draycott's hat was blown off and Green leapt off the trap to recover it. Mr Draycott attempted to turn the horse around, but the animal backed them into the New Cut River which was swollen to flood by the rain; there was at least 11ft of water in the stream and the Draycotts were thrown into the water. The strong current swept Mrs Draycott and her child away, both drowned and their bodies recovered from the waters the following day. Mr Draycott almost suffered the same fate, but was pulled clear by Green.

26 OCTOBER 1853

Posters appeared around Soham and Ely displaying instructions of what to do to avoid the threat of cholera:

Observe the strictest cleanliness both in person and dwellings. Avoid all chances of being chilled and keep the body warm, particularly the stomach, bowels and feet.
Avoid placing the feet upon the cold floor.
Abstain from sleeping on the ground or with windows open.
Avoid the cold and damp of the night air.
Avoid excess fatigue.
Whatever may be the weather or the season, do not go too lightly clad.
Sobriety cannot be too highly recommended.
Abstain from undressed food of every description and especially unripe fruit.
All cold drinks, when a person is heated, are dangerous. Instead of drinking pure water mix it with two teaspoons of brandy to a pint.
Excessive use of strong liquors is highly dangerous and taking unmixed brandy, when fasting, is equally so.
All beer and cider of bad quality should be avoided.
Every person who feels himself suddenly affected by dull pains in the limbs, heaviness of giddiness in the head – a feeling of oppression, uneasiness about the chest, heartburn or cholic should immediately apply to a Physician.
Persons thus affected, should immediately go to bed and take, quite hot, an infusion of peppermint and heat himself by every possible means.
If a bowel complaint comes on take from 20 to 50 drops of laudanum in hot brandy and water and go into a hot bed.

27 OCTOBER 1899

Thomas Lucas (41) was brought before Cambridge Assizes indicted for the attempted murder of his wife Mary by shooting her at Coveney on 7 July. On the night in question Mrs Lucas had gone to bed taking her two young children with her because there was a thunder storm and they were frightened. Thomas Lucas had returned home at 10 p.m.

and told the boys to go to their own room; he showed the boys a light then brought his gun into the bedroom. Standing at the foot of the bed he pointed the gun at his wife. She pulled the bedclothes over her head but Lucas pulled them down and again levelled the gun at her. She raised her left arm to protect her head. He then shot her; the main blast was taken by her arm. He then said, 'I will go and have the other myself'. He left the room and the gun was heard to discharge another shot. Help was obtained and Mrs Lucas was taken to Addenbrooke's Hospital, where her shattered arm had to be amputated.

Lucas was found in a corn field and arrested the following morning; one of his cheeks was injured by shot. Lucas claimed he had perpetrated his acts while drunk, he claimed he only took the gun into the room to frighten his wife, but others gave evidence that the man had ill-treated her and had threatened to kill her on a number of occasions. At the trial the defence argued that the gun had gone off accidentally and that Lucas had forgotten it was loaded. Lucas was lucky, the jury found him guilty of wounding with intent. The judge agreed with their verdict but also stated that, 'the prisoner's dastardly act was to be the last of a long series of acts of cruelty.' Lucas was sentenced to twelve years' penal servitude.

28 OCTOBER 1899

Charles Dennis begins the first full day of his sentence in prison. He had been found guilty of setting fire to a stack of wheat straw at Fordham on 28 July. Mr Justice Wills said, 'it was a most wanton and wicked thing to do. It was a most dangerous crime.' He sentenced Dennis to four years' penal servitude.

29 OCTOBER Strange Tales and Folklore of Cambridgeshire: Spit a Sixpence

One Fen lore that lingered in the Burwell area was the sure fire test of anyone suspected of having committed a crime. After confrontation, if they could 'spit a sixpence' (i.e. spit enough to cover a sixpence) their innocence was considered proved. Equally, if a murderer was confronted by evidence proving his crime, it was said his finger tips would drip blood.

30 OCTOBER 1913

The Wisbech Riot. On this day the news of Dr Horace Dimock's death after taking an overdose was broadcast in Wisbech. He had been drafted in to help clear the case load of doctors willing to work under the terms of the 1911 National Insurance Act. The poor of Wisbech rapidly took the kindly doctor to their hearts, but his arrival was met with hostility from some of the other doctors. Soon the other GPs were receiving hate mail supporting the work of Dr Dimock and criticising them. Dr Meacock received particularly aggressive and obscene postcards 'containing not only written matter but sketches also' sent anonymously through the post. He informed the police and Dr Dimock was arrested on a charge of criminal libel. Brought before the magistrates, Dimock was remanded on bail. Returning to his parents' farm at nearby Stretham, he died at noon on 27 October; a bottle containing veronal tabloids was found under his pillow.

When news of his death reached Wisbech, a crowd soon gathered and rushed to Dr Meacock's house by the river, jeering, and sang 'He's the cause of all the rouble, cause of all the strife' and stoned the windows; the crowd then proceeded to Dr Gunson and a stone was thrown, breaking a window. Dispersed from this area the crowd massed again at the Clarkson memorial, where fireworks were thrown at the police. The local police could not cope and had to call for reinforcements.

After two days of sporadic disturbances, ever-increasing numbers of protestors and even more windows being smashed at the doctors' houses, enough was enough and in desperation the mayor formally read the Riot Act and the crowd dispersed when the police went in with truncheons drawn. Several persons received nasty blows and some women were knocked down and trampled on, but no cases of serious injury were reported. The mob protests may have been put down but Wisbech remained unquiet for a long while afterwards.

31 OCTOBER

All Hallows Eve. A night for ghoulies, ghosties and long-legged beasties! Probably the most famous of all East Anglian ghosts is the great spectral dog known predominantly as Black Shuck. Over the years Shuck has been seen at numerous locations across Cambridgeshire, where the beast is believed to be an omen of bad luck to all who hold it in their gaze, some say the dog brings a curse and that if you see him either you or a member of your family will go mad or die within the year; the only way to break the spell is not to tell a soul what you saw for a year and a day.

The Black Shuck, the Devil Dog of the Eastern Counties.

Among the recorded sightings, Shuck has been seen bounding along the Lark Bank at Prickwillow in the direction of Ely, and across the fields and road between Braham Farm and Witchford; loping around the ancient earthworks at Arbury and Wandlebury as well as at Soham, Parson Drove, Snailwell, Upware, between Whittlesea and Coates, and at Spinney Bank between Wicken Fen and the Spinney marshes. At this last location, during the twentieth century a woman was severely shocked after seeing Shuck by the 'black draining mill'. She described the 'black dog' as coming along the Spinney Bank, 'quiet as death' and 'big as a calf'. It was padding along with its head down, and its 'gret old ears flappin', then, when it was no more than 20yds away, it raised its head and glared at her, with 'eyes red as blood'. She was 'laid up' for a week with shock. Another woman was not so lucky and the shock of seeing the beast sent her to an early grave.

In his book *Ghosts and Witches*, J. Wentworth Day wrote:

> A curious variation of this ghostly hound is said to haunt an overgrown and little-used lane called Slough Hill in the parish of West Wratting ... Police Constable A. Taylor, of The Tiled House, Panton Street, Cambridge, tells me that, in his youth, this lane which is on the road from West Wratting to Balsham was haunted by an extraordinary thing called 'the Shug Monkey.' It was, he says, 'a cross between a big rough-coated dog and a monkey with big shining eyes. Sometimes it would shuffle along on its hind legs and at other times it would whiz past on all fours. You can guess that we children gave the place a wide berth after dark!'

Sightings of Black Shuck in the East Anglian countryside can be found recorded in sources of great antiquity, other more local stories account for the manifestation of their area. In his youth Mr W.H. Barrett was told of a big black dog whose master was drowned one foggy night when his horse ran down the river bank and plunged into the Great Ouse, half-way between Littleport and Brandon creek. On pitch-black nights wayfarers could hear Shuck padding along the road whining and howling for his dead master. Barrett recalled, 'Some even declared that they had felt the dog's hot breath against their legs, while people living in the houses alongside the road dreaded the dark nights when Shuck's howls kept them awake as he roamed up and down the river bank.'

However, it was claimed this particular Shuck's existence was ended very abruptly in 1906. A well-known Littleport resident was motoring home one foggy autumn evening when he crashed into some object on the road and stalled his engine. He landed off the road and with his front wheel only a few feet from the river at the very spot where Shuck's master had been drowned 100 years before. The animal was never heard again, so this accident must, the local folk declared, have been the first case of a ghost dog being run over and killed by a motorcar.

NOVEMBER

The locked door of a lumber room in Caius College was finally opened on 9 November 1789; the problem had been that the Revd Samuel Reeve MA, Fellow and Senior Proctor of the University, was the only person to have a key and he had not been seen since 1 July. He was found inside hanging by the neck. The jury returned a verdict of lunacy; he was buried at St Michael's on 11 November.

1 NOVEMBER 1613

Worst recorded floods at Wisbech occurred. An inscription on the east wall of the Church of St Peter and St Paul commemorates the following:

> To the immortal Praise of God.
> Be it in memory, that on the 1st Nov. 1613, in the night, the sea came in by the violence of a north-east wind, meeting a spring tide, and overflowed all Marshland with the Town of Wisbech, both on the North and South Sides, and almost the whole Hundred round about, to the great danger of mens' lives, with the loss of some by the breach of banks, &c. besides the spoil of corn, cattle, and houses, which could not be estimated.
> The year after, on the 23rd of March, it was then again overflowed by the fresh water, which came by a great snow, that not only the South Side of this Town, but the greater part of the ground within South Eau Bank in Holland, from Spalding to Tyd St Giles, was almost lost for that year; with a great part of Marshland, from their bank called the Edge, between their Towns and the Smeeth to their new Podike, by divers breaches between Salter's Lode and Downham Bridge.

2 NOVEMBER

Feast of All Souls, Commemoration of all the Faithful Departed. In a masterful piece of storytelling Sir Arthur Grey, under the name of Ingulphus related the strange tale of *The Everlasting Club* (1919). The Club's minute book spanning the years 1738 –1766 was in the hands of the master of Jesus College. Grey related the following:

> Its number was limited to seven, and it would seem that its members were all young men, between 22 and 30. One of them was a Fellow-Commoner of Trinity: three of them were Fellows of Colleges, among whom I should especially mention a Fellow of Jesus, named Charles Bellasis: another was a landed proprietor in the county, and the sixth was a young Cambridge physician. The Founder and President of the Club was the Honourable Alan Dermot, who, as the son of an Irish peer, had obtained a nobleman's degree in the University, and lived in idleness in the town. Very little is known of his life and character, but that little is highly in his disfavour. He was killed in a duel in Paris in the year 1743, under circumstances which I need not particularise, but which point to an exceptional degree of cruelty and wickedness in the slain man.

Eight laws of the Club were then listed, the most significant being Rules 6:

> On the Second day of November in every year, being the Feast of All Souls, at ten o'clock post meridiem, the Everlastings shall meet at supper in the place of residence of that Corporeal member of the Society to whom it shall fall in order of rotation to entertain them, and they shall all subscribe in this Book of Minutes their names and present place of abode.

And Rule 7:

> It shall be the obligation of every Everlasting to be present at the yearly entertainment of the Society, and none shall allege for excuse that he has not been invited thereto. If any Everlasting shall fail to attend the yearly meeting, or in his turn shall fail to provide entertainment for the Society, he shall be mulcted at the discretion of the President.

The rest of the rules, Grey explained, 'were either too profane or too puerile to be quoted.' Over the years, tragedy, fate and strange ends claimed the lives of all the members of the Everlasting Club, all that was except Charles Bellasis:

On the night of November 2nd, 1766, a terrible event revived in the older inhabitants of the College the memory of those evil days. From ten o'clock to midnight a hideous uproar went on in the chamber of Bellasis. Who were his companions none knew. Blasphemous outcries and ribald songs, such as had not been heard for twenty years past, aroused from sleep or study the occupants of the court; but among the voices was not that of Bellasis. At twelve a sudden silence fell upon the cloisters ... In the morning all remained quiet about Bellasis' chamber. When his door was opened, soon after daybreak, the early light creeping through the drawn curtains revealed a strange scene. About the table were drawn seven chairs, but some of them had been overthrown, and the furniture was in chaotic disorder, as after some wild orgy. In the chair at the foot of the table sat the lifeless figure of the Secretary, his head bent over his folded arms, as though he would shield his eyes from some horrible sight. Before him on the table lay pen, ink and the red Minute Book. On the last inscribed page, under the date of November 2nd, were written, for the first time since 1742, the autographs of the seven members of the Everlasting Club, but without address.

The entrance to the room used for the sinister congregations of the Everlasting Club.

3 NOVEMBER 1853

Cholera outbreak in Isleham. In the Report from the General Board of Health on 9 November it was recorded:

> There has been an outbreak of the epidemic in this large village, Dr Waller Lewis, who on hearing of the occurrence at once proceeded there, states that '... it is in the most deplorable condition. Great numbers of the people live in large hollows in the ground, from which many years ago building stone was extracted. In one pit there are nearly 500 people in a state of great deprivation and dirty in the extreme. In the first house I entered one corpse had just been placed in a coffin, another poor child was nearly ready for his last narrow resting place, and a third had a fair chance of recovery. Six deaths had already occurred, and the medical officer had between 30 and 40 severe cases on his hands. The number of inhabitants is between 2,000 and 3,000. There is but little medicine and not one druggists shop in the village, which is 5 or 6 miles from the nearest town ... Few private houses are provided with privies, and there are but four public necessaries, which have not been cleared out for nearly two years.

4 NOVEMBER 1913

Execution of Frederick Seekings (39) at the County Gaol, Cambridge, the last execution to take place in the county. Seekings was a labourer of Brampton, an ignorant man and 'a demon in drink.' He had been living with Martha Jane Beeby for a number of years – their arguments, fought after heavy drinking sessions, were well known in the village.

Monday 28 July 1913 was the Brampton Feast Day; Seekings had finished work and arrived at the Bell Inn at about 8 p.m. Martha joined him later and they staggered out together and Seekings was seen pushing Martha in a hedge, more than once. At about 11 p.m. Ernest Favell and Edward Abraham left the festivities to go home. At Favell's house his wife said someone had been 'rumbling about the house.' Mr Favell went for his cycle lamp and walked out along the Thrapston Road. Within 100yds they discovered the prostrate bodies of Seekings and Beeby, he lying across the lower part of her body with his left arm around her legs. Closer examination proved she was cold to the touch, deathly cold; the light of the lamp revealed her throat had been slashed across.

The police were sent for. Seekings was very drunk but alive; when challenged about what had happened he stated, 'I didn't do it. She took the knife away from me and done it herself.' In his left trouser pocket they found the murder weapon, a closed clasp knife, still smothered in blood.

At his appearance before the magistrates, Seekings claimed, 'I was worse for drink or I should not have done such a thing, if I did do it I don't remember doing it.' Brought before the assizes the jury were convinced that he was culpable, and returned their 'guilty' verdict after just fifteen minutes. Mr Justice Bray sentenced Seekings to death, a sentence carried out at 8 a.m. precisely on this day by Thomas Pierrepoint.

5 NOVEMBER 1827

Guy Fawkes Night has always been a night for revelries and mischief among the Cambridge undergraduates. In 1827 John Simpson Redhead, Charles Willimott, Samuel Bowman, James How, William Glover, Robert Burrows, Charles Edwards and James Raby all ended up before Lord Chief Justice Best charged 'for having, with others, assaulted the Proctors and other officers of the University, in the execution of their duty.'

The discovery of Frederick Seekings slumped over the body of Martha Beeby.

Charles Willimott was acquitted, but the others were all found guilty and sentenced to terms of imprisonment varying from one to twelve months. In 1904 the mischief went too far. After taking an undergraduate into custody PC Broughton was set upon, brutally attacked by a group of others, kicked to the ground and left insensible. Broughton was sent to a convalescent home for two months, but medical experts had to conclude the injuries he had suffered to his spine were such he could not work again. This fine young constable, once tall and strong was now 'crippled and doubled up.' He was granted a pension of full pay, at £1 5s 7d a week.

6 NOVEMBER 1842

A fire was discovered on the roof of a large barn on the farm of John Fyson at Woodhurst. The barn soon burned to the ground and the blaze rapidly spread to nearby buildings and corn stacks. The St Ives fire engine was soon on the scene, but due to high winds and scarcity of water it was of little use and soon eleven thatched cottages downwind of the fire were ablaze. County Magistrates concluded it had been caused by an accident after labourers had entered the barn with lanterns; one of them carried a broken lantern with a candle.

High jinks by undergraduates on 5 November in the early twentieth century.

A local tale recounts how some of the village labourers appeared indifferent to the blaze as some were drunk and 'engaged in pugilistic contests.' Perhaps one of the men had sparked off the fight by saying, 'I warned you not to use that broken lantern.'

7 NOVEMBER 1750

A double execution took place at Ely. The assizes had heard two apparently unconnected murders committed at Whittlesea where both killed their spouses. The first case was that of John Vicars, a man from a family who 'lived in good credit.' He had married Ann Easom, but she was said to have been a sickly woman whose temperament was not helped by her illness. Vicars went off and joined the Army, only returning again upon receiving news of her death about a year later.

Vicars then began a relationship with Mary Hainsworth. Vicars was not keen to marry again, but Mary kept on pleading and persuading him she would make him a good wife. She then got nasty and threatened him with a warrant if he would not marry her. They did marry and seemed to rub along happily enough for a few months, but then the arguments grew more frequent and intensified; there was also physical violence and jealousy in their Whittlesea home.

One day Vicars saw his wife in the shop her mother had provided for her and, the *Newgate Calendar* explains:

> His resentment got the better of his reason. Stepping into the shop where she was sitting at work, and placing his left hand under her chin and attempt to cut her throat, but was prevented by her putting her hands up when she felt the knife. He then placed the point of the knife under her left ear, the back part upwards, and stuck it downward as they stick sheep. She once cried: 'Murder!' He said: 'Molly, it is now too late; you should have been ruled in time.'

John Vicars lunges murderously at his wife Mary at Wittlesea.

He then ran into the street and called out for somebody to take him prisoner. Thomas Boone took hold of his arm, and he surrendered himself. While in prison Vicars wrote his confession. He freely admitted his guilt at the assizes, his only request being that he should be able to see the execution of Amy Hutchinson first; this favour was granted by the court.

So what happened to Amy Hutchinson? She was newly married to John Hutchinson, but he was not the love of her life; that was Thomas Reed, but he had been deemed unsuitable and never received her father's blessing. By the time of her marriage Reed had left the village, but he returned when he heard of the wedding. Amy could not resist her old paramour and was soon involved in covert meetings with him. These liaisons soon got back to John, he challenged her, they argued and, fuelled with drink, he beat her.

Almost seven weeks to the day after their wedding, John Hutchinson died after a short 'illness'. His death was not treated with undue suspicion and he was buried on 16 October. The trouble was, Amy did not observe a decent amount of widowhood and began living with Reed and gossips wondered why Amy had bought arsenic shortly before her husband's death. On 18 October Amy was arrested and removed to Ely

The rope from the Cambridge gallows.

Gaol; the body of John Hutchinson was exhumed the following day. The post-mortem examination showed evidence of 'corrosive medicine' in his stomach. They gave some of 'the same liquor mucus' from the stomach to a dog, which died seven hours later.

When Amy was brought before the assizes she swore her innocence. Witnesses testified to Hutchinson's violence towards her, but there was also those who told of her adulterous behaviour and some careless comment she had been heard making to others about how she wanted to 'get shot' of her husband. Found guilty as prescribed under the laws of petty treason Amy was sentenced to be burned at the stake.

On the morning of their execution John Vicars behaved very steadily, but penitent, as he took his place on the gallows. He prayed with the minister. Amy Hutchinson was then brought out:

> ... her face and hands being smeared with tar, and having a garment daubed with pitch, after a short prayer the executioner strangled her, and twenty minutes after the fire was kindled, and burned half-an-hour. He went then to Vicars, who very undauntedly helped him to fix the knot, and immediately threw himself off, and expired in a few minutes.

8 NOVEMBER 1879

Robert Henry James (20), a labourer, was brought before the Cambridge Assizes indicted for the manslaughter of Mary McIntyre at Cambridge. The story revealed by the hearing told how James had attempted to pick a fight with William McIntyre, the son of the deceased, on 27 September. William declined and went into his house. James followed and burst through the door. Standing immediately behind that door was 84-year-old Mrs McIntyre; she was knocked down and fell against the bed. She complained of being injured, but no harm was visible. The following day Surgeon Knowles examined the woman, there was tenderness to the side of the ribs but he did not detect there was one broken. On 13 October the poor woman was removed to the workhouse infirmary in great pain, the medical officer examined her but detected no breaks. She died on 30 October. The post-mortem did reveal one of her ribs was broken; the cause of death was recorded as bronchitis. Found guilty of manslaughter, Robert James was sentenced to twelve months' imprisonment with hard labour.

9 NOVEMBER 1879

Robert Allen (20) begins the first day of his sentence in Cambridge Prison. Brought before the assizes charged with highway robbery with violence, it transpired he and another man had stumbled out of a public house at Eversden on 8 October, both of them in an inebriated state. After about a mile up the road, Allen tripped up his compatriot and kicked him while on the ground, threatening to kill him and throw him over the hedge. As the man lay on the ground, Allen rifled his pockets for the purse he had spotted the man had in the pub. Allen claimed he had only picked the man out of the ditch and left him by the side of the road, he swore he did not take the purse. It was proved that Allen had been seen after the attack with the purse and two half-sovereigns his victim had claimed were in it. The jury convicted Allen of larceny only, but with a previous conviction against him Allen received ten months' imprisonment with hard labour.

10 NOVEMBER 1866

Did the chores get too much for her? Reports were published of the inquest held at the Plough, Elsworth, before F. Barlow, Esq., into the death of Ann Newman. Her husband was a labourer and had risen at about five o'clock, and said to Ann that he would fetch some water, to which she replied, 'No don't, I shall not want any.' He went to work and thought nothing more of this apparently ordinary day at his toils. Upon his return at seven o'clock in the evening he found the door locked. No call, shout or knock at the door could rouse his wife from within so the door had to be broken open. Inside, a pail of water and kindling stood upon the floor, but no fire burned in the grate. Nobody was found downstairs, so it was with a great sense of impending tragedy the journey was made upstairs. Ann was found hanging from a beam from which she had suspended herself by a piece of bed cord. She was quite dead. The jury returned a verdict that she 'destroyed herself' while in a state of temporary insanity.'

11 NOVEMBER 1858

Drink driving is nothing new. A fatal accident occurred near Quy Bridge on the Newmarket Road, Cambridge. Susan Butler (23) was enjoying a day with her friend Sarah Walker of Chesterton. They had already had a drink when they caught a flyer to the Plough at Fen

Ditton, and, rather scandalously, smoked cigars as they went along! At the Plough they drank some more and met two gownsmen, who invited them for a drive in their trap.

Susan wanted to drive, the men tried to persuade her against it, but she took the reins and would not give them up. She drove at a sensible speed at first but as they neared the turnpike she whipped up the horse and drove through the gate at a gallop. She turned on the high road toward Cambridge then back through the Newmarket Gate toward Bottisham. The gentleman beside her tried to take the reins, but she would not relinquish them. Near the Quy bridge, there was a cart close to the trap, they felt a jerk, there was a crash and the occupants were thrown out instantly. The other occupants managed to get up, but Susan remained groaning on the ground. She died a short while later without regaining consciousness. Outwardly she scarcely had a mark upon her except a faint scratch down one side of her face; post-mortem revealed she had hit her head in the fall and died of 'concussion of the brain'. The Coroner's jury returned a verdict of 'accidental death.'

12 NOVEMBER 1930

John McEwan of Glasgow and Joseph Greaves of Bolsover are held on remand at Peterborough. They had entered the Palace Picture House on 7 November with the intention of blowing open the safe, which contained nearly £100. They failed so miserably to force the safe in any way they called the police. Upon arrival of the boys in blue the two handed over the box of gelignite and said they were so disgusted at not being able to open the safe they decided to telephone the police to arrest them.

13 NOVEMBER Tales from the Gaols: Hard Labour

Hard Labour was a familiar addition to sentences such as manslaughter or for crimes which carried short sentences but merited extra punishment, such as aggravated theft, brawling or repeat offenders. Typical types of hard labour were: the treadmill, shot drill, stone breaking and the crank.

Shot drill entailed a prisoner having to lift single cannonballs (weighing up to 14.5kg) up to chest height, carry it a set distance and make a pile, repeating the process until the set number of cannonballs had been moved in like manner. In the larger prisons up to fifty convicts could be engaged in 'shot drill'; they would be formed into three sides of a square and standing three deep and 3yds distant from each other. Each end of the open square would have a neat pile of cannonballs which would be picked up one at a time and then passed from man to man and from one end to the other. The exercise would be repeated for a standard hour and a quarter.

Stone breaking was particularly favoured in the prisons near quarries like Dartmoor or Portland; this soul-destroying task saw the convict smash a set number or weight of stones with a sledgehammer until the boulder was reduced to such fine gravel it would pass through the sieves.

14 NOVEMBER Strange Tales and Folklore of Cambridgeshire: The Cambridge Oak

From Hone's *Every-Day Book* (1826):

> According to 'T.N.', a Cambridge correspondent, the Willow tree is, in that county, called the Cambridge Oak. Old Fuller calls it 'a sad tree, whereof such who have lost their love make their *mourning garlands;* and we know that exiles hung up their harps upon such doleful

supporters. The twigs hereof are physick to drive out the folly of children. This tree delighteth in moist places, and is triumphant in the *Isle of Ely*, where the roots strengthen their banks, and top affords fuell for their fire. It groweth incredibly fast, it being a by-word in this county, that the profit by willows will buy the owner a horse before that by other trees will pay for his saddle. Let me add, that if *green ashe* may burne before a queen, *withered willows* may be allowed to burne before a lady.' The old saying, 'She is in her willows' is here illustrated; it implies the mourning of a female for her lost mate.

15 NOVEMBER 1777

The gentlemen of St John's College, soon after dinner was ended in the hall, were suddenly alarmed by a great number of sportsmen of the Old Walden Hunt riding full speed into the great court, in pursuit of a stag, which had taken refuge in one of the staircases.

16 NOVEMBER 1833

An arson attack at Chatteris was reported in *The Times*: 'Thursday the 7th inst., between 9 and 10 o'clock, a most alarming fire broke out in a straw stack, on the premises of Mr William Curtis of Chatteris Mill End near the road leading to Somersham.' Fire engines were soon on the scene, but the high winds carried the flames to a barn containing deals and wheat, some hovels and more stacks of hay and corn; all were soon consumed.

Another fire was discovered on the following Sunday on the side of the road out of Chatteris, a small wheat cob that belonged to Mr H. Wright, the surgeon, was destroyed. A third blaze was discovered the following Wednesday in a row of corn stacks on the premises of Mr John Seward of Chatteris at Whom Farm. The fire engines succeeded in preserving the barn, two stacks of oats and an oat cob, but the rest were destroyed.

Two young labourers, local lads named Skeels and Boss, were suspected of starting the fires and brought before the magistrates. They were committed pending trial; one was detained at Ely Gaol, the other at Wisbech.

17 NOVEMBER 1870

Dr William Tubbs, who practiced at Parson Drove and later at Outwell, died. In the days when anaesthetics were dangerous and unproven anyone who could provide safe pain relief for surgical procedures would be cheered a hero; Dr Tubbs was one such man and he used mesmerism (now commonly known as hypnotism) to render his patients insensible. He wrote a number of papers and articles on his methods. Witnesses attested to the effectiveness of his methods, including a variety or procedures as diverse as the removal of 'a firm molar tooth' from a young man of 23 to the removal of the diseased breast of a 'respectable married woman.' He was buried with the respect and regret of his neighbours, and upwards of 1,000 mourners followed his funeral cortège to his grave at Upwell.

18 NOVEMBER Strange Tales and Folklore of Cambridgeshire: Wife Selling

In 1933 Dr Charles Lucas recorded an incident 'some years ago' and still remembered by some local people – the sale of a wife at Swaffham Bulbeck. The story told of how one November day two tinkers arrived in the village; in the afternoon, bill posters were circulated announcing a public auction at the Royal Oak inn. The auctioneer opened the proceeding and announced he had had to offer 'a most desirable lot' and a woman was led in with a halter around her neck and stood on a footstool so all could get a good look at her. The auctioneer then described the 'lot' as: red nose, thick lips, bent back, receding chin and eye where one 'looks straight at you, the other wanders up to the North.' The bidding began at sixpence and the hammer went down at half-a-crown and she was sold to the companion of the tinker who was selling her.

19 NOVEMBER 1768

Edward Mallett was executed on the Ely gallows for stealing a horse.

20 NOVEMBER 1881

A fatal affray occurred at the Cambridge Lunatic Asylum. The inmates had breakfasted as usual and were sent to the wards. An altercation arose between a young man named Warwick from Cherry Hinton and an elderly gentleman named Taylor from Carlton; both had been in the asylum for a number of years. Taylor struck Warwick a violent blow to the jaw and walked away. Warwick recovered himself and hit back at Taylor with a severe blow under the right ear. The attendant arrived just as Taylor was reeling and saw him fall to the ground. Dr Bacon, the medical superintendent, and Mr Boyd his assistant were summoned, but within minutes Taylor was dead.

21 NOVEMBER 1807

A reward of 2 guineas was offered for information leading to the apprehension of Job Harley and William Eaton, both from Littleport. They had absconded leaving their families chargeable to the parish. This was far from a rare occurrence; men would simply walk out on their families and as there was no social security payment in those days, needy families would fall upon the parish to support them. Hence a reward would be offered for the apprehension of such people; it would have saved the parish a lot more money in the long run.

22 NOVEMBER 1893

A shocking accident occurred to Mr Ebenezer Sykes. He was driving home from Peterborough to Whittlesea with a friend when, during an awkward turn near the river, the horses ran into an iron fence. The occupants of the trap were thrown out; Sykes fell on his head and rolled into the river. His friend urged him to swim, but there was no reaction. When the body of Sykes was recovered it was found his neck had been broken by the fall.

23 NOVEMBER 1791

A duel arising from 'a trifling dispute' was fought near Newmarket between Mr Applewhaite and Mr Rycroft, students of Pembroke Hall. Mr Rycroft was so severely wounded he died on 25 November. Mr Applewhaite and Mr Hollond of Trinity College, the second of the deceased, were expelled. The following notice was published by the Vice-Chancellor:

Whereas it has been represented to the Vice-Chancellor, that some students in the University have been observed shooting at marks with pistols, an exercise which obviously tends to introduce and promote the dangerous and impious crime of duelling; it is hereby publicly declared, that if any person in statupupillari shall be discovered in the exercise of so unwarrantable and dangerous a practice, he will be proceeded against as guilty of a very high offence, and be liable to the severest penalties mentioned in the forty-second statute.

24 NOVEMBER Report of the Prison Inspectors

Cambridge Town Gaol, 1853:

Number of Prisoners at time of Inspection: 34 Males, 12 Females and 6 Debtors.

There was a slight increase in the number of commitments, principally, I am sorry to observe, in the number of prisoners committed to trial for serious offences. The buildings were in good order. The ventilation and drainage have been considerably improved. The division wall in the corridor of the female ward has been removed. There has been no alteration in the clothing, bedding or the diet; the provisions were of good quality. The daily cost of the food was 4*d* per head. The general health of the prisoners has been good. No prisoner was sick on the day of inspection; neither had there been any death or removal on medical grounds during the year. The late chaplain having resigned, the Mr Barham has been appointed to succeed him. He has been twelve months in office, and states: 'I have great satisfaction, notwithstanding the lamentable ignorance which prevailed among the majority of the prisoners, I have found them almost without exception willing to receive instruction, and apparently grateful for the means I employed for their reformation.'

The general conduct of the prisoners has been satisfactory. The punishments awarded for prison offences were: Males 19, Females 1. There were no offences of a grave character.

Cambridge Town Gaol in the nineteenth century.

All the repairs and alterations within the prison have been executed by the prisoners; they are also employed mat making, picking coir and oakum and in making and mending the prison clothes and shoes. The clear profit on work done for sale during the year was £32 9s 4d and the estimated value of the work done was £83 3s 2d.

The provisions, fuel and stores are supplied by contract. The net cost per prisoner last year, exclusive of any charge for repairs was £20 3s 2d.

The separate system has now been two years in operation in this prison and has produced a great change in the conduct of the prisoners, not only while under restraint within the walls but the Governor refers to one or two cases of prisoners who, having been subjected to the discipline for a period of one year, are living honestly and respectably since their discharge, giving satisfaction to their employers. The chaplain also speaks with much confidence of the effect of the discipline. The prisoner 'John Newitts' who has now been 11 years confined in the prison, has conducted himself better during the past year, but is still subject to occasional fits of excitement.

25 NOVEMBER 1878

Henry Gilbert (40) was executed on the Huntingdon gallows for the murder of his illegitimate child, Henry Colbert Gilbert, at Hail Weston on 21 September 1878. The story was a simple one and the task for the jury was to decide if the death of the child had been caused by accident or murder.

Henry Gilbert was living with Ann Colbert and their child as husband and wife; he was a labourer on Mr Pentelow's farm, she worked as a servant in the farmhouse. Ann had left her employment upon discovery of her pregnancy and moved in with Gilbert the previous July. On the night of the child's death Gilbert had returned at about 8 p.m. He had been drinking, but was not drunk. Upon entry he enquired after the baby, which had been suffering from whooping cough, gave Ann his wages and instructed her to get some shopping in the village. He went up to bed; the babe was asleep on a mattress on the floor. Upon her return, Gilbert called, 'Ann, bring a light; I think the baby is dead.' Rushing upstairs she found Gilbert cradling the baby in his arms. There was blood all over his shirt and over the bedclothes; Gilbert claimed he had suffered a nosebleed.

The police were called and Gilbert claimed he was concerned the child was choking and because there was no light he may have hit the child's head on a box as he picked it up. A close examination of the baby's head showed extreme violence had been used. At the inquest and in court the doctor was certain more than one blow had been inflicted upon the child, causing the fatal effusion of blood in the head, and he could not believe they were inflicted accidentally. The judge, Mr Justice Hawkins, summed up 'with great care and at considerable length'; the jury retired and found Gilbert guilty of murder, but recommended him to mercy. The death sentence was passed. In the condemned cell Gilbert admitted the crime, but claimed he did not intend to commit murder. He was hanged at Huntingdon by public executioner William Marwood.

26 NOVEMBER 1774

A report appeared in the *Cambridge Chronicle* concerning the tragic case of three poisonings in the household of Mr Crabb at Littleport. His granddaughter, her companion and a maid servant had all been poisoned while sampling their concocted remedy for 'the itch'.

27 NOVEMBER 1703

Cambridge citizens begin to clear up after the previous night's storm. Described at the time as 'the greatest storm ever known in England,' the daylight revealed the extent of the damage:

> Part of King's College Chapel fell down; part of Katherine's Hall New Chapel was damnified; fifteen stacks of chimnies fell down into St John's College, without hurting any body, but two or three miraculously escaped. St Peter's College was much damnify'd, and a stack of chimnies fell into the Vice-Chancellor's chamber but was so far from hurting that he was not awaken'd by it.

28 NOVEMBER 1910

Mrs Douglas Crossman (38) was killed in a fatal hunting accident. The wife of the master of the Cambridgeshire Hounds had set out from the meet at Eltisley Wood and had run about four fields when her horse, in taking a fence at the Caxton Steeplechase, struck the top and fell on its rider, breaking her neck.

29 NOVEMBER 1886

William Norman a gamekeeper in the employ of Mr G.O. Newman of Croxton Park was on the main road leading from St Neots to Cambridge at 5.30 in the afternoon when he heard a gunshot in a plantation of his land, where he knew there to be pheasants. He hid in a ditch and observed three men he recognised as local poachers, namely Alfred Carr, Joseph Jeffs and Samuel Barnes, leaving the area.

Norman attempted to apprehend Jeffs and struck him with a spud. In reply Barnes hit the keeper with his gun barrel, an action that caused the gun to explode. Although the shot did not affect Norman, he was knocked down, Jeffs stuck him a violent blow with the spud, saying he would 'ram it down' his throat, then threatened to kill Norman. Carr was not seen to strike Norman; he dissuaded his confederates from further violence, but did not interfere to prevent injury to the keeper. After receiving a beating over a fifteen to twenty-minute period the poachers walked away, leaving Norman collapsed on the road.

Once they had gone he managed to get to the head keeper's cottage in an almost fainting condition. Medical examination revealed extensive bruising over most of Norman's body, cuts to his hands and his right arm fractured close to the wrist. The three poachers were tracked down, arrested and brought to trial at the Huntingdon Assizes in January 1887.

Despite the pleas for leniency on behalf of Carr, the judge was aware he had been convicted of poaching on a number of previous occasions and found them all guilty of unlawful wounding. Jeffs received five years' penal servitude while Barnes and Carr were sentenced to eighteen months' imprisonment with hard labour.

30 NOVEMBER 1885

The last judicial beheading in England. In the annals of crime and punishment it is rare that the execution of the criminal becomes more infamous than the crime itself – this is one of those rare exceptions. Robert Goodale (45), a man prone to getting drunk and making threats took it a fateful step further and attacked his wife with a billhook.

A violent exchange between gamekeepers and poachers.

The recovery of the body of Bathsheba Goodale from the well on her family smallholding on the Walstoke Marshes.

*A fanciful depiction of the
end of Robert Goodale.*

He thought he had killed her and put her body down the well at their smallholding on Walsoken Marsh near Wisbech, where she drowned.

Brought before the Norwich Assizes, he was found guilty and sentenced to death. The date set for his execution was Monday 30 November 1885. Executioner James Berry observed Goodale was a man of large frame, but he had wasted away while in prison. According to the 'table of drops' Goodale would require a drop of 7ft 8in, but Berry was not happy with this length, Goodale's neck was 'not very muscular' so Berry shortened the drop to 5ft 9in. The surgeon asked Berry if he thought this was enough of a drop to avoid strangulation, Berry assured him it would be.

On the morning of the execution Goodale was brought onto the gallows and the final preparations were made. Berry pulled the lever, the traps fell open and Goodale was plunged to eternity. Berry recorded what happened next in his memoirs: 'We were horrified, however, to see the rope jerk upwards and for an instant I thought the noose had slipped from the culprit's head or that the rope had broken.' The governor, surgeon and Berry looked into the pit below. Berry continues:

> ... having feared the noose had slipped off Goodale's head ... it was worse than that for the jerk had severed the head entirely from the body and both had fallen into the bottom of the pit ... the Governor, whose efforts to prevent any accident had kept his nerves at full strain, fairly broke down and wept.

Although acquitted of any blame, the 'Goodale Mess' haunted Berry for the rest of his career and probably for the rest of his life. Reporter Charles Mackie recalled the execution when he looked back on his career many years later. With quite some pride he declared he had been present at what could quite justifiably be called 'the last judicial beheading in England.'

DECEMBER

HOUSE OF CORRECTION, ELY.

RULES AND REGULATIONS.

Convicted Prisoners sentenced to Hard Labour.

1. The Governor shall enforce a high degree of cleanliness in the prison, as well as respects every part of the building and yards, as the persons of the prisoners, their clothing, bedding, and every thing in use; and the prisoners shall conform to such regulations for that purpose as the Governor may lay down.

2. Every prisoner shall wash himself thoroughly at least once every day, and his feet at least once each week.

3. Every prisoner, unless he is excepted by the Medical Officer, shall go into a warm bath at least once in each month; but no prisoner shall be bathed or stripped in the presence of any other prisoner.

4. The hair of female prisoners shall not be cut except when the Governor thinks it necessary on account of vermin or dirt, or when the Surgeon deems it requisite on the ground of health; the hair of male prisoners shall not be cut except for the purpose of health and cleanliness; they shall be shaved at least once a week.

5. Every prisoner shall be supplied with clean linen, including shirt, stockings, and handkerchief, at least once in every week.

6. No boy under 14 years of age, shall, under any circumstances, be placed on the tread-wheel; and no prisoner shall be placed on the tread-wheel, or put to hard labour, without the previous sanction of the Medical Officer. Twelve thousand feet shall be the maximum height which any one prisoner shall ascend on the tread-wheel in any single day.

7. Every prisoner shall be employed, unless prevented by sickness, at such hard labour as can be provided, and for so many hours, not exceeding ten, as the Governor may direct; he shall not be allowed any portion of his earnings, neither shall he receive any extra allowance in consequence of any labour performed by him.

8. If the Governor shall at any time deem it improper or inexpedient for a prisoner to associate with the other prisoners of the class to which he may belong, he may confine such prisoner with any other class of prisoners, or in any other part of the prison, until he can receive directions respecting the case from a Visiting Justice.

9. Gaming of every kind is prohibited in the prison, and among every description of prisoners.

10. Every prisoner shall regularly attend Divine Service in the prison chapel whenever it is performed, unless prevented by illness or properly excused.

11. Prisoners of this class shall not be allowed to see their friends and relations until after the expiration of the first three months; but subsequently to that period they may receive visits in the course of each successive three months; they may also see their legal advisers, on an order from a Visiting Justice, and send and receive one letter in the course of each quarter of a year.

12. The Governor shall inspect every letter to or from a prisoner, except such as are addressed to a Visiting Justice or other proper authority.

13. He shall, at all times, be ready to receive any complaint or application of a prisoner; and he shall cause any article of food to be weighed or measured if so required by any prisoner.

14. He shall have power to hear all complaints touching any of the following offences: that is to say,—disobedience to the rules of the prison; common assaults by one prisoner upon another; profane cursing and swearing; indecent behaviour, or any irreverent behaviour at chapel; all of which are declared to be offences if committed by any description of prisoners; absence from chapel without leave; idleness or negligence in work, or wilful damage or mismanagement of it; which are also declared to be offences if committed by any prisoner under charge or conviction of any crime. He may examine any person touching such offences, and may determine thereupon; and may punish all such offences by ordering any offender to close confinement in a refractory or solitary cell, and by keeping such offender upon bread and water only for any term not exceeding three days; but he shall not determine any of these cases without previous examination; neither shall he delegate his authority in these matters to any other person. No punishments or privations of any kind shall be awarded except by the Governor or by a Visiting or other Justice.

15. In case any criminal prisoner shall be guilty of any repeated offence against the rules of the prison, or shall be guilty of any greater offence than the Gaoler or Keeper is by this Act (4 Geo. IV., c. 64) empowered to punish, the said Gaoler or Keeper shall forthwith report the same to the Visiting Justices, or one of them, for the time being; and any one such Justice, or any other Justice acting in and for the county, or riding, or division of a county, or for the district, city, town, or place to which such prison belongs, shall have power to enquire, upon oath and to determine concerning any such matter so reported to him or them and to order the offender to be punished by close confinement, for any term not exceeding one month, or by personal correction, in the case of prisoners convicted of felony, or sentenced to hard labour.—4 Geo. IV c. 64, s. 42.

16. Silence and regularity will at all times be strictly enforced, and each prisoner placed in his own cell during meals and on the Sunday (except during the time of Divine worship), provided that every prisoner shall be allowed as much exercise in the open air as the Surgeon may deem necessary for health.

Rules for the House of Correction, Ely, c. 1860.

1 DECEMBER Cambridgeshire Death and Burial Rites

Joseph Hannath bought the hall at Tydd St Giles in 1812. He lived there for the rest of his life, but his wife predeceased him. He was so heartbroken when his wife died that he kept her body in the house for six weeks until he finally relented and allowed her to be buried. Her ghost is said to walk house.

2 DECEMBER Report of the Prison Inspectors

Cambridge Borough police station, 1853:

> The police station has been removed to the buildings adjoining the spinning house; these buildings afford ample accommodation for the police and cells for the prisoners. I suggested some alterations with a view to give more light and ventilation in the passages.
> The number of prisoners confined during the year was 402 which is 72 below that of the preceding year; of these 48 were committed for trial; 187 were summarily convicted and 167 were discharged. The cells were clean and in good order.

3 DECEMBER Strange Tales and Folklore of Cambridgeshire: The Gogs

The Gog Magog Hills near Stapleford are said to be the resting place of the ancient British giants Gog and Magog – I do not say *final* resting place as many folk tales say they are just sleeping.

T.C. Lethbridge claimed to have discovered a group of hidden chalk carvings in these hills after using a sounding bar to identify soft areas which he claimed indicated where the chalk had been cut away. Lethbridge believed the carving he had found to be a depiction of Epona, the Celtic horse goddess. Weeks of excavations and soundings revealed more. The three-breasted Goddess not only travelled across the side of Gog Magog with her beaked horse but she also pulled a chariot and it soon became apparent that she was not alone. Two additional figures on either side of the goddess were plotted by Lethbridge. On one side was a warrior with sword and shield on the other a curious figure wearing a cloak. The two warriors and the goddess were different in artistic style; Lethbridge concluded that the central figure had been constructed by the Iceni and represented the Magog, or Mother God, known as Epona to the Celts while the other two figures were later additions crafted by the incoming Catuvellauni tribe. Lethbridge's discoveries, described at length in his book *Gogmagog: The Buried Gods* (1957), remain the subject of much debate.

However, the figures on the hill were not pure invention, the first published reference to their existence is by Bishop Joseph Hall in 1605, when he described a 'picture the Schollers of Cambridge goe to see at Hogmagog Hills,' supposedly of a giant known as 'All Paunch'. In 1640, local historian John Layer commented: 'I could never learn how these hills came to be called Gog Magog Hills, unless it were from a high and mighty portraiture of a giant witch the Schollars of Cambridge cut upon the turf ...' Antiquarian William Cole (1714–1782) also recalled a 'figure of the giant carved on the turf.'

4 DECEMBER 1788

A report was published concerning the case of Thomas Adkin, who had been prosecuted by Cambridge University for an assault he perpetrated upon James Wood, fellow of St John's, at the Union Coffee House in the town. He had suffered judgement by default and was brought before the King's Bench and fined £100. Adkin offered to make an apology in the Senate House, but refused to sign an apology for insertion in the public papers.

5 DECEMBER 1926

The *Sunday Express* publishes the account told by Lieutenant-Colonel Foley relating his experiences of a haunted room in Corpus Christi College in October 1904. The manifestation was that of an 'invisible, but tangible thing, or being, which sometimes became dimly visible, inhabiting or visiting this room.' Four students had entered the room and one of them was dragged away from the others. His companions grabbed him, but something continued to pull him away from their grasp 'like some powerful magnet.' The students pulled their friend away from the force and had to fight what soon became a frenzied battle with the unseen force to eventually release him from its powerful hold. Other students heard the commotion from within the room, gained entry and crowded into the room and wrecked it, even tearing down some of the oak panelling, but no physical cause of the occurrence was discovered.

6 DECEMBER 1728 Grim Tales of Cambridgeshire: Dead Ringer

In December 1728 Henry West, the bell ringer of King's College, was crushed to death by one of the five great bells of the college.

7 DECEMBER 1833

John Stallan, the arsonist fireman, was executed in front of the county gaol. Stallan had been brought before the assizes on charges of having set fire to a barn at Great Shelford. When first accused he had blamed his wife, claiming she had confessed the matter to him and even told him how she rolled up balls of rags and straw and thrust them into the thatch of the barn to set them alight to ensure the barn well and truly 'went up'. However, he was not believed, and was found guilty at the assizes and sentenced to death. Once there was no chance of reprieve, Stallan gave up his protestations of innocence and wanted to clear his mind; he confessed to the fire he was convicted of, and added he had caused another eleven. He explained he had no malice towards any of the owners of the fired properties, his only aim in starting the fires being the 6s 6d he would earn as a fireman attending the blazes!

On the morning of his execution Stallan took the Sacrament, but declined to take formal leave of his fellow prisoners, instead he addressed some words to them, pointing out the consequences of a sinful life as exemplified by his own case. Of his final moments on the gallows it was recorded: 'He was much exhausted on reaching the scaffold and required support. He died almost without a struggle although the high wind which prevailed caused the body to sway about, and produce a contrary opinion.' After an hour the body was cut down and removed to Shelford for burial.

8 DECEMBER 1881

A prisoner in Cambridge County Prison made a 'desperate attack' upon Mr Sexton, the head turnkey. The prisoner had borne malice against the warder and took an opportunity when he knew the door leading to the prison yard was locked, to cut off the bell communication by breaking the wire. Then, when in the room alone with the officer, he seized a chain with a ring at the end and struck the warder a violent blow on the head, knocking him unconscious. Sexton's wife came running followed by their child; they were also hit by the violent convict. The door key was thrown out of a back window and soon the warders entered and after a brief struggle secured the prisoner.

9 DECEMBER 1911

The body of Mr J.W. Crabtree, a member of the Wisbech Town Council, was recovered from the River Nene. He was driving home in his Humber car from a Masonic gathering at March when, a couple of miles outside Wisbech, the car ran into the river near the Redmore Sluice. The following morning a passer-by noticed a cap and a cushion floating down the river and the hood of a motorcar protruding 2ft out of the water. The tide was high and it was not possible to remove the car until later in the day. The body was later recovered from the river.

10 DECEMBER Strange Tales and Folklore of Cambridgeshire: Weathering the Fens

As the cold of the winter began to bite, the Fen folk would often find it hard to keep warm. Their cottages were often simple wattle and daub affairs, thatched with reeds from the fen; many suffered with damp; one writer in 1763 found most cottages on the area of the Fen he visited 'ankle deep in water' from almost perpetual flooding. Legend would have it that because of their constant life in water Fen Tigers developed webbed feet and even took on the same colourations as eels. One thing is for sure, there was a lack of fuel; there was a scarcity of trees on the fens and peat turves were expensive (in 1730, 700 would sell for 4s 6d), so many fen folk resorted to burning dried cattle dung to keep their home fires burning.

11 DECEMBER 1885

Reports were published concerning the 'violent and dangerous conduct' of Radicals at the elections in Littleport. A Mr Lyon, who was engaged in an official capacity around the polling booths, narrowly escaped injury when stones were thrown. Then, when he left the polling station, he was mistaken for Captain Selwyn, the Conservative candidate, and was then stoned all the way home.

12 DECEMBER Punishments of the Past: The Country Lock-Up or Cage

Up until 1840 every parish was required by law to provide a 'lock-up' or 'cage' for the temporary detention of prisoners arrested by the parish constable. In Cambridgeshire, like most English counties, lock-ups came in a number of shapes and sizes; some were brick and slat board, others all brick. In the main they looked like enlarged privy houses with a reinforced door and an unglazed window fitted with bars or an iron grill.

Most lock-ups had just one cell about 8 or 10ft-square and were built on waste ground in a public part of the village, often in close proximity to the stocks and whipping post. Some lock-ups were larger and had two cells for such requirements – as separate cells for men and women – or for keeping brawlers apart. In practice lock-ups were mostly used as cells where the drunk and disorderly were thrown in for the night and let out in the morning, when they had sobered up.

The village lock-up on Overcote Lane, Needingworth.

Some of the surviving examples of lock-ups in the county can be found at Needingworth, Coveney and Fen Drayton. One of the last recorded uses of a Cambridge lock-up was in 1912, when a local policeman put a drunken man into the Trumpington lock-up to sober up. The following morning the policeman unlocked the door and found the man just as drunk as the night before. It appeared his confederates had inserted a rubber tube through the vent in the cell and kept him well 'topped up'!

13 DECEMBER 1776

Littleport is a filled with talk of the assault and drowning of Rebecca Crabb in a ditch near the bridge. Two local men were suspected of the crime. One of the men, William Gotobed, surrendered himself a few days later and was committed to Ely Gaol to await trial. At the assizes the following March he was acquitted of the murder, but the stigma of the accusation haunted him for the rest of his days.

14 DECEMBER 1876

Robert Browning was executed at Cambridge Prison for the murder of fifteen-year-old prostitute, Emma Rolfe. Browning (25) was a journeyman tailor. On 24 August he had gone with the girl on to Midsummer Common near the Maid's Causeway, Cambridge. PC Joseph Wheel of the Borough police heard a shriek from across the common and, as he walked to investigate, he came across Browning who gave himself up as a killer after being challenged about what he was doing. Browning produced a razor from his pocket; it was still wet with blood. Browning claimed he had bought Emma some ale but she had then she had robbed him of a shilling. No money was found on her body or near the spot.

Browning's defence attempted a plea of insanity – the jury were far from convinced and almost instantly returned the 'guilty' verdict. Despite a plea for mercy on account of his age, Browning was to keep his appointment with the hangman. When all hope of reprieve was lost he wrote his confession in the condemned cell.

15 DECEMBER Strange Tales and Folklore of Cambridgeshire: Dead Men's Shoes

A long-held belief among the Fenland river lightermen was that shoes taken from a dead man's feet would bring good luck. An old saying at Lode also referred to your fate being determined by how the wear on the soles of your shoes manifested:

Wear it at the ball – live and spend all
Wear it at the heel – spend a good deal
Wear it at the side – live and thrive.

16 DECEMBER 1863

Suspicious mind. Brought before the assizes was the case of William Carter of Whittlesea who, as a consequence of 'some fancied or assumed provocation' on the part of his wife, Harriet, kicked her, struck her across the face and then attempted to murder her with a reaping hook he had been sharpening. A surgeon commented after seeing the amount of blood she had lost as a result of her wounds that she was lucky to be alive. So severe were the wounds that she still bore the scars when giving her testimony in court. William Carter defended his actions by saying his wife's misconduct had

MURDER AT CAMBRIDGE.

Robert Brown, stands charged with the murder of Emma Rolfe, by cutting her throat with a razor, on a Common near Cambridge, on Thursday night, Aug. 28th, 1876. The Prisoner has confessed the crime to Police Constable Wheel.

The victim was an "UNFORTUNATE GIRL,"

Tune:—Driven from Home.

: o :

In the quiet town of Cambridge a deed has been done,
That I'm sure has surprised and startled each one ;
An unfortunate woman but just in her prime,
Alas ! is the victim of this cruel crime.
Well known in Cambridge, from virtue betrayed,
In the path of dishonour too early she strayed ;
But whatever she's been we can all understand,
Her life was as sweet as the best in the land.

CHORUS.

Poor Emma Rolfe had no time to repent,
On Midsummer common to eternity sent ;
Robert Brown was her murderer, in prison he's cast.
From virtue she strayed to be murdered at last.

God only knows what a hard life she led,
The sale of her honor was the price of her bread ;
Exposed to the scoffs and the jeers of the world,
Her short life was passed, in deep misery hurled.
In cheap gaudy clothes obliged to dress gay,
Poor women like her their days pass away ;
They must wear a smile tho' the heart is sick and sore,
Till they go to their graves and are heard of no more

She met with her murderer on Thursday night,
They both went together soon after twilight ;
They went to the common for a purpose we know,
They quarrelled and then he gave her a death blow ;
He then cut her throat with a razor so keen,
The poor woman's blood on the pathway did stream,
Her sad wretched life, alas ! it was o'er,
Ere the morning had dawn'd, Emma Rolfe was no
more.

A policeman was brought and the murderer confess'd,
For the crime he committed he now has no rest,
He would give all the world to recall that sad hour,
But what has been done is beyond earthly power.
She was murdered that night, with her sins on her
head,
We hope they're forgiven now she's laying dead ;
Tho' lost to the world, despised and forlorn,
Someone will miss the poor girl now she's gone.

Robert Brown will be tried for this unmanly crime,
And if he's found guilty must suffer in time ;
We pity his brother and relations as well,
Who are grieving for him as he lies in his cell :
His poor victim lies in her cold narrow be,
Never no more to her ruin be led ;
Young girls beware you are not led astray,
For plenty will quickly decoy you away.

Don't be too hard on this poor woman's fate,
She might have reformed, but now it's too late
Perhaps she had no one to snatch her away,
To save her from ruin or going astray :
When the first step is taken 'tis hard to return,
Many a poor girl this sad lesson must learn,
And many a kind mother has had a dear child,
By some wealthy young flatterer to ruin beguiled.

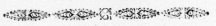

London :—H. P. SUCH, Machine Printer & Publisher
177, Union-street, Borough, S.E.

The broadside sold at the time of the execution of Robert Browning, December 1876.

been such that his home was 'wretched'. The jury found Carter guilty of unlawful wounding and he was sentenced to ten years' penal servitude.

17 DECEMBER 1853

Keep your hair on! Reports were published of a near-fatal accident that befell Mr George Murdan, a carpenter of Elsworth. Having travelled to Cambridge with his timber-gig for some wood, upon his return journey, when very close to home, one of the horses suddenly snatched forward and threw him to the ground; the wheel of the vehicle narrowly missed his face but ran over his scalp, literally tearing the hair from his head. The report concluded, 'we are glad to say the poor man is progressing very favourably.'

18 DECEMBER 1824

Thomas Savage was executed on the Huntingdon gallows. Savage (22), with two other miscreants named Cook and Wood, had had a few drinks and talked up some mischief, specifically setting fire to a building in the town. They had all conspired, but it seems it was Savage who actually struck the match that set Martin Wellman's barn ablaze, the fire spread and about twenty houses were lost.

Soon after the incident, Savage was heard bragging about the items he had looted. This reached the ears of the local constable and soon all three were arrested and imprisoned. Cook and Wood turned King's Evidence and Savage was left to hang. He was taken to his place of execution by cart, a journey he shared with the coffin that was to contain his body. After spending some moments kneeling in prayer by the box, he then sat on it and made the most of his last moments waving to the crowd as he passed by.

19 DECEMBER 1831

Mister Popularity or the Riot at Bassingbourn. Many local men were unemployed and the future prospects of employment did not look good as one farmer already had a threshing machine and cheap Irish labour was also being used on the land. The local men wanted action, a deputation was assembled and they went to see James Unitt, the farm foreman, to see if he could devise a plan for their employment. He made an arrangement with his boss and a few other local dignitaries to meet at the Bull to see what could be done.

The men from the village got wind of this meeting and were loitering in a group in the street. As time progressed more joined them from the surrounding area and they soon became quite an unruly mob. Mr Unitt was shouted at and abused as he passed through the crowd but made it into the pub safely, however in a short time tempers flared in the mob and the doors and windows of the pub were broken as the labourers made their entry. It was reported that: 'the women were particularly active, among them Martha Cubiss who, armed with a spade, swore she would have Mr Unitt's brains out; another was provided with a fire shovel which she brandished with great wrath.' Mr Unitt was then set upon by the labourers, 'knocked about', carried into the kitchen and given a thorough kicking. This done he was then removed to the street, his coat was torn from his back and he was further pelted with all manner of vile road detritus from rocks and stones to dung, and persecuted with cries of 'Murder him! Burke him! Take him to the horse-pond, and finish him!'

It was estimated that the mob numbered some 250 people. If villagers attempted to offer Unitt a place of safely the mob blocked him each time he approached a friendly door. Poor Mr Unitt, he said if he could only have addressed them he had no doubt he could convince them that he was deserving of their kindness – not their enmity. But Mr Unitt would not be heard and he was pummelled and pelted over at least 2 miles distance before he could get away. He was 'bruised from head to heel' and was confined to his bed for three days as he recovered from his wounds.

Thomas Hopes, William Dockrell, Thomas Cubiss, Martha Cubiss and John Harroden were all brought before the assizes and found guilty for their active participation in the riot.

20 DECEMBER 1879

Typhoid fever was reported on this date to be very prevalent in Soham, with no fewer than twenty cases on Quy Fen Common. Measles and low fever were likewise prevalent, but reports from the locale were quick to point out 'every precaution was being taken.'

21 DECEMBER Cambridgeshire Death and Burial Rites

In 1903 Emily Josephine Jepson of Union Lane, Cambridge obtained a patent for her ...

> ... Improved Coffin for Indicating Burial Alive of a Person in a Trance or Suffering from a Comatose State so that same may be released or rescued, has means for admitting air to the coffin and for giving audible signal by means of an electric bell, which may be placed either on the grave or in the cemetery house. There is a glass plate in the lid, and a small shelf attached to one side of the coffin which may hold a hammer, matches and candle so that, when the person wakes, he can light the candle and with the hammer break the glass plate, thus assisting to liberate himself when the earth above the coffin is removed.

22 DECEMBER 1841

PC Thomas Saunders Lamb reported for duty at 7 p.m. for night duty at Huntingdon. During the night colleagues who encountered Saunders saw in him nothing out of the ordinary in his mood or demeanour. Lamb's last orders were to keep an eye on the Rising Sun pub for a drunk. He left in that direction and that was the last time the constable was seen alive. He did not report at the end of his shift and a search was made in the daylight, but there was no trace to be found of him. On 1 January 1842 PC Lamb's top hat was found near the bank of the river at Hartford; just over a month later on 16 February the body of PC Lamb, still in his uniform, was recovered from the river at Huntingdon and carried to the nearby Windmill public house. There were no signs of violence upon his body, even the post-mortem found nothing untoward. It was soon assumed by many the constable had committed suicide.

The death of PC Lamb would not lie quietly. In 1867 a convicted forger named John Negus, wanted to clear his conscience (and perhaps attempt to reduce his sentence) by making a statement to the effect that he had seen William Shippey, his sons Edmund and William Shippey jnr and his wife along with a fourth man he thought to be the landlord of the Fleece dragging the semi-conscious PC Lamb, his head on one side, to the bridge, where they dropped him in the water.

Edmund Shippey was traced and brought to trial; he pleaded 'not guilty,' but had spoken candidly 'I am thinking of my neck swinging.' The distance of time was against Negus, so was his criminal record. The jury were not convinced and Edmund Shippey was fully acquitted and the death of PC Lamb remains a mystery. His truncheon is displayed in the Norris Museum and his ghost is said to walk the bridge.

23 DECEMBER 1818

Burial at the Melbourn crossroads. Until the 1850s people who committed suicide could not officially be buried in consecrated ground, but were interred in a separate, distant area in the north of the churchyard where the body would be laid face down, facing west. Many believed the restless spirits of suicides would 'walk' to harass those they left behind, so they would be buried away from the population at a four-way crossroads so the ghost would not know which path to take to return. To ensure the body and ghost stayed down, it would often be chained and 'pinned' with an oaken stake through the heart (a practice only prohibited by Act of Parliament in 1823).

Edward Neaves had been found hanging from a bed post in his lodging-room, following an inquest held before coroner John Ingle Esq at Melbourn on this day in 1818, and after a long investigation, the jury unanimously returned a verdict of *felo de se*. The coroner, therefore, directed his warrant to the proper officers to cause the body to be buried in some public highway, and it was accordingly deposited near the direction post at the south end of the parish of Melbourn, leading to the town of Royston. Crowds would gather around the local sexton as he performed this duty at the wayside grave, even children would risk the wrath of their parents by creeping along and looking through the legs of those assembled at the grim rite.

24 DECEMBER

The Lord of Misrule. Recorded on this day in *The Book of Days* the Lord of Misrule played an important part in Christmas Festivities in the past. His duties were to act as the Master of Ceremonies at the multifarious revels of the season. In the University of Cambridge, the functions of the Lord of Misrule, known there as the *Imperator* or *Præfectus Ludorum*, were performed by one of the Masters of Arts, who was regularly elected to superintend the annual representation of Latin plays by the students and take charge over their boisterous seasonal games and diversions.

25 DECEMBER 1661

Huntingdon shopkeeper and Quaker, Robert Raby, opened his shop on Christmas Day; he was joined by other Friends from his local religious community. Outside the shop a crowd of locals gathered. Disgusted at their apparent disregard of this Holy Day, they pelted the Quakers with 'Dirtt and Mire'. Unfortunately for Mr Raby, his windows and shutters were open.

26 DECEMBER Punishments of the Past: The Spanish Mantle

Folk drinking to excess and becoming unruly is nothing new. In the seventeenth and eighteenth centuries the judiciary employed a simple punishment for habitual drunkards. Removing the base of a barrel and cutting holes for head and arms to poke through, the culprit was made to wear 'The Drunkard's Cloak'; the penance was enforced by a metal collar locked around the offender's neck, by which he would be led by a Beadle or law official around the town.

THE LORD OF MISRULE.

27 DECEMBER Cures of Fenland Cunning Folk: Cure for Lethargy

In 1802 Dr W. Butler of Clare Hall, Cambridge was called to the house of a local clergyman. It appears the man of God had become so stressed over the sermon he was to preach before the king he could no longer sleep. His friends had advised him to take opium and the man took so much 'it threw him into a profound lethargy.' At this point Dr Butler was summoned and upon learning the circumstances he flew into 'a violent passion' and warned the clergyman's wife she was in danger of being hanged for killing her husband and left the room to return home quickly, followed by the pleading wife. As he passed through the yard he saw several cows and, after ascertain the cows belonged to the clergyman, the doctor said, 'Will you give me one of those cows if I can restore him to life?' She agreed, the doctor ordered the cow to be killed and the reverend patient put into the warm carcass, which in a short time completely revived him!

28 DECEMBER Grim Tales of Cambridgeshire: The Cambridge Black Museum

The most notorious of all museums is the Black Museum of crime relics in Scotland Yard, but all over Britain smaller collections of the macabre may be found on display or in private hands. One collection that existed for many years was that of Mr Edwin Rutter. It was located at the rear of his tailors business in the Olde Curiosity Shop on Trumpington Street, opposite the Fitzwilliam Museum, and entitled 'The Cambridge Museum of Prison, Punishment and Royal Relics.'

Among this remarkable collection were relics such as keys, handcuffs, leg shackles, wrist crushers and thumb screws from London's notorious Newgate Prison. There was also a scold's bridle, Georgian truncheons, knuckledusters, a spiked ball and chain used by rioters in the Lenten Bread Riots of 1780, some of Dick Turpin's clothes and effects that were once displayed in the Three Tuns pub, a whipping post and whip, cat o'nine tales, three continental execution swords and the ropes used in the executions of the Norwich murderer William Sheward and John 'Babbacombe' Lee – the man they could not hang; there were even photographs of the executioners that used them. The star attractions, however, were the relics from the old Cambridge Prison, which included the doors of the condemned cell and entrance gate to the place of execution, and even the execution scaffold and trap doors.

Sadly the collection was divided up and sold off, but many of the artefacts from this remarkable museum are still known and treasured in private black museum collections all over the world.

29 DECEMBER Grim Tales of Cambridgeshire: Adulterated Milk

Josiah Hunter, cattle dealer of Hungate House, Wisbech was summoned before the Guildhall in London in December 1895 for selling adulterated milk – in other words he had added water to it to make it go further. Food adulteration was a common crime and could be inflicted on a vast array of groceries and drinks from bread, flour and coffee to milk and beer. This crime was truly despised as the goods affected constituted the basic necessities for the poorest people. It was summed up in this popular ditty:

> Little drops of water added to the milk
> Make the milkman's daughter clothe herself in silk.
> Little grains of sand in the sugar mixed
> Make the grocery man soon become well fixed.
> Little acts of meanness, little tricks of trade,
> All pass for keenness, fortunes thus are made.

Hunter had been suspected for some time. When he was caught the milk he had supplied to Messrs F. & T. Gibson in London had 25 per cent added water, in previous tests it had been diluted by up to 32 per cent. It was believed Hunter would have made a profit of about £40 over the time he had supplied Gibson's. Hunter pleaded 'guilty', but swore he could not ascertain how the water had come to be added. Hunter blamed his staff and sacked them all. Hunter was fined £10 and 3s 6d costs.

30 DECEMBER Grim Tales of Cambridgeshire: Daddy Witch

Daddy Witch was an 'ancient bony creature, half clothed in rags, who lived in a hut by the sheep pond in Garret's Close, Horseheath.' She was known and feared throughout the area. If work went wrong, animals misbehaved or crops failed many would pay her a few shillings to break the spell. Daddy Witch died in 1860 and her familiars, white mice named Bonnie, Blue Cap, Red Cap, Jupiter and Venus were collected by a person described enigmatically as 'a lady from Castle Camps.' Daddy Witch was buried in the middle of the road leading from Horseheath to Horseheath Green. Even years later the belief in the power of Daddy Witch remained; the area was always marked by its dryness, believed by some to have been caused 'from the heat of her body.' Children and numerous adults acknowledged the site of Daddy's grave well into the twentieth century. In July 1935 it was recorded that a fire spreading along the road stopped short of the grave, turned and went over the fields.

31 DECEMBER 1774

A report in the *Cambridge Chronicle* stated that on Saturday evening at about six o'clock, George Hall, a tailor from Melbourn, was returning home from Cambridge market with provisions for his large family, when he was attacked in the portway, about half a mile from his own house by two stout fellows, who demanded his money. When he refused they knocked him down, one of his assailants knelt on his body, while the other robbed him of 27s 6d. The account continues:

> ... after he was at liberty he remonstrated against their baseness, saying that they were rogues indeed to rob such a man as he was; on which with horrid imprecations they ran after him, and in all probability would have murdered him, had not his fright furnished him with an agility that outstripped them, and he got safe home, leaving behind him his hat, and a leg of mutton, which were afterwards found by the neighbours in the cartway.

SELECT BIBLIOGRAPHY

BOOKS

Arthur, Jane, (ed.) *Medicine in Wisbech and the Fens* (Wisbech, 1985)

Bell, John, *Cambridgeshire Crimes* (St Ives, 1994)

Bell, John, *More Cambridgeshire Crimes* (St Ives, 1995)

Blakeman, Pamela, *Ely Prisons* (Ely, 2001)

Bruce, Alison, *Cambridgeshire Murders* (Stroud, 2005)

Cambridgeshire Federations of Women's Institutes, *The Cambridgeshire Village Book* (Newbury, 1989)

Cash, Arthur Hill, *Laurence Sterne: The Later Years* (London, 1986)

Chambers, Robert, *The Book of Days* (London, 1869)

Cooper, Charles Henry, *Annals of Cambridge* volume IV [1688–1849] (Cambridge, 1852)

Cooper, John William, (ed.) *Annals of Cambridge, by Charles Henry Cooper* volume V [1850–1856], with additions and corrections to volumes 1–4 and an index to the complete work (Cambridge, 1908)

Dring, W.E., *The Fenland Story* (Cambridge, 1967)

Dugdale, William, *History of Imbanking and Drayning* (London, 1662)

Harper, Charles, *The Cambridge, Ely and King's Lynn Road* (London, 1902)

Harries, John, *The Ghost Hunter's Road Book* (London, 1974)

Hippisley Coxe, A.D., *Haunted Britain* (London, 1973)

Hone, William, *The Every-Day Book and Table Book* (London, 1826)

Howat, Polly, *Ghosts & Legends of Cambridgeshire* (Newbury, 1998)

Keatinge Clay, William, *A History of the Parish of Waterbeach in the County of Cambridge* (London, 1859)

Kirby, R.S., *Kirby's Wonderful and Eccentric Museum* (London, 1820)

Lane, Brian, *The Murder Club Guide to the Eastern and Home Counties* (London, 1989)

Notestein, Wallace, *The History of Witchcraft in England 1558–1718* (Washington (DC), 1911)

Porter, Enid, *Cambridgeshire Customs & Folklore* (London, 1969)

Rossell Hope Robbins, *The Encyclopaedia of Witchcraft and Demonology* (Feltham, 1959)

Richings, Derek and Rudderham, Roger, *Strange Tales of East Anglia* (Seaford, 1998)

Rouse, Michael, *Spinney Abbey* (1971)

Rudderham, Roger, (compiled by) *Littleport Chronicle* (Wisbech, 1981)

Storey, Neil R., *A Grim Almanac of Essex* (Sutton, 2005)

Storey, Neil R., *A Grim Almanac of Suffolk* (Sutton, 2004)

Storey, Neil R., *A Grim Almanac of Norfolk* (Sutton, 2003)

Summers, Montague, *The Geography of Witchcraft* (London, 1927)

Tatem, Moira, *The Witches of Warboys* (Cambridge, 1993)

Timpson, John, *Timpson's England* (Norwich, 1997)

Toulson, Shirley, *East Anglia: Walking the Ley Lines and Ancient Tracks* (London, 1979)

Ward, Philip, *Cambridge Street Literature* (Cambridge, 1978)

Wedlake Brayley, Edward, *The Beauties of England and Wales* (London, 1808)

Wentworth Day, James, *Here are Ghosts & Witches* (London, 1954)

Wentworth Day, James, *In Search of Ghosts* (London, 1969)

PERIODICALS AND JOURNALS

Cambridge Chronicle

Cambridge Independent Press

Cambridge Intelligencer

Country Life

Daily Mirror

East Anglian Magazine

Fenland Notes and Queries

Ely Gazette

Ely Standard

Fortean Times

Huntingdonshire County News

Proceedings of the Cambridge Antiquarian Society

Reynolds News

The Times

Whittlesea Chronicle

Wisbech Advertiser

Wisbech Standard

Other local titles published by The History Press

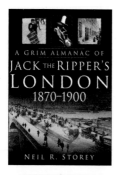

A Grim Almanac of Jack the Ripper's London 1870-1900

NEIL R. STOREY

Have you ever wondered what the London that witnessed the Jack the Ripper murders was really like? If you have, then enquire within. This almanac explores dreadful deeds, macabre deaths, strange occurrences and grim tales from the darker side of the capital's past. If it's horrible, if it's ghastly, if it's strange, it's here — and if you have the stomach for it, then read on ...

978 0 7509 4895 3

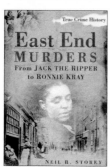

East End Murders

NEIL R. STOREY

Neil R. Storey has drawn on a vast array of original sources — among them witness statements, coroners' reports and court records — to produce a revealing insight into the East End's darkest moments. As well as the murders of Jack the Ripper, perhaps the most infamous in history, he looks as nine other cases in detail including the still mysterious Ratcliffe Highway Murders of 1811 and the unsolved murder of Frances Coles in 1891.

978 0 7509 4668 1

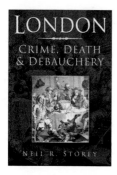

London: Crime, Death & Debauchery

NEIL R. STOREY

London: Crime, Death & Debauchery is an alternative history of the darker side of Britain's capital city. No other book on London covers this topic in such a complete fashion, with cases ranging from the Restoration to the early nineteenth century. It weaves macabre accounts into an entertaining criminal history accessible to all.

978 0 7509 4624 7

Cambridgeshire: Strange But True

Robert Halliday

This book explores people, places and incidents that are unusual, odd or extraordinary. We discover the truth behind 'Hereward the Wake', the story about the originator of the expression 'Hobson's Choice', a woman who spent nine days trapped in a snow cave, and many more tales of local characters, curious events and strange traditions. Illustrated with a range of photographs, maps, prints, paintings and engravings, Robert Halliday tells an alternative history of Cambridgeshire that will fascinate residents and visitors alike.

978 0 7509 4059 7

Visit our website and discover thousands of other History Press books. **www.thehistorypress.co.uk**